Observing Organisations

In order to prevent or solve problems within organisations, one needs not only to address the conscious elements but also to understand the unconscious aspects.

Observing Organisations presents a unique approach derived from direct participant observation of small units within institutions, all in the health and social services sector. A range of contributors bring together the results of their own observational projects – in settings as diverse as a mental hospital canteen, an acute psychiatric admission ward and a palliative care unit – to show how they were able to come to a psychoanalytically informed understanding of the cultures that arise within health care organisations. Such an understanding may be used to overcome difficulties that arise within the organisations.

Observing Organisations will help all health care workers, teachers and managers better understand the functioning and difficulties of their organisations and therefore help in the management and practice of their work.

R.D. Hinshelwood is Professor in the Centre for Psychoanalytic Studies at the University of Essex, and was previously Clinical Director of the Cassel Hospital, London. **Wilhelm Skogstad** is a Consultant Psychotherapist at the Cassel Hospital and a psychoanalytic psychotherapist in private practice.

Observing Organisations

Anxiety, defence and culture in health care

Edited by R.D. Hinshelwood and Wilhelm Skogstad

With a Foreword by
Anton Obholzer

London and Philadelphia

First published 2000 by Routledge
11 New Fetter Lane, London EC4P 4EE

Simultaneously published in the USA and Canada
by Taylor & Francis Inc.,
325 Chestnut Street, Philadelphia, PA 19106

Routledge is an imprint of the Taylor & Francis Group

Typeset in Times by Mayhew Typesetting, Rhayader, Powys
Printed and bound in Great Britain by Biddles Ltd, www.biddles.co.uk

British Library Cataloguing in Publication Data
A catalogue record for this book is available from the British Library

Library of Congress Cataloging in Publication Data

Observing organisations : anxiety, defence, and culture in health care / edited by
Robert D. Hinshelwood and Wilhelm Skogstad.
    p.   cm.
Includes bibliographical references and index.
ISBN 0–415–19629–9 – ISBN 0–415–19630–2 (pbk.)
1. Health facilities—Administration—Psychological aspects. 2. Health services
administration—Psychological aspects.   3. Health care teams—Psychological
aspects. I. Hinshelwood, Robert D. (Robert Dayles), 1938–   . II. Skogstad,
Wilhelm, 1952–   .

RA971 .O27 2000
362.1'068—dc21   00–022355

ISBN 0–415–19629–9 (hbk)
ISBN 0–415–19630–2 (pbk)

Contents

Contributors

Marco Chiesa, MD (Milan), MRCPsych, is Consultant Psychiatrist in Psychotherapy at the Cassel Hospital, Richmond, Surrey, Hon. Senior Lecturer at University College London and a Member of the British Psycho-Analytical Society. Until recently he was Senior Tutor in Psychotherapy and Hon. Consultant Psychotherapist at The Institute of Psychiatry and the Maudsley Hospital, London. He has been particularly involved in, and has published about, psychoanalytic research.

Flavia Donati, MD (Milan), Associate Member of the Italian Psycho-analytic Society, practices in Rome as psychiatrist and psychoanalyst. From 1980–9 she worked in London in psychiatric hospitals and in a residential therapeutic community.

Judith Edwards, MRCPsych, did a speciality training in psychotherapy at the Cassel Hospital. She is particularly interested in a psychoanalytic approach to the understanding and treatment of psychotic disorders. She is currently working in Forensic Psychiatry.

R.D. Hinshelwood, FRCPsych, is a Member of the British Psycho-Analytical Society. He is Professor in the Centre for Psychoanalytic Studies, University of Essex, UK and was previously Clinical Director of the Cassel Hospital. He initiated and supervised this observational work at St Bernards Hospital, London and the Cassel. He has written extensively on therapeutic communities and on Kleinian psychoanalysis, including *A Dictionary of Kleinian Thought*, and *Clinical Klein*. His most recent book is *Therapy and Coercion: Does Psychoanalysis Differ from Brain-Washing?*. He was the founder of *The British Journal of Psychotherapy*.

Debbie Maxwell, BA, LSSM, is an independent stress management consultant and a member of the Society of Stress Managers. She has recently completed a Masters degree in the Psychoanalysis of Groups and Organisations at the University of Essex. Her background is in business, she works as a design and management consultant for private organisations in the commercial sector undergoing processes of change.

Mark Morris, BA, MBChB, MRCPsych, is the Director of Therapy at Grendon Underwood and an Associate Member of the British Psycho-Analytical Society. He did his medical and psychiatric training in Glasgow, worked for a year in the Barnet Psychiatric Crisis Team and as a Senior Registrar in Psychotherapy at the Cassel Hospital and then as a Consultant Psychotherapist at St Bernards Hospital in London.

Noreen Ramsay, trained as a psychiatrist with a special interest in the psychological problems facing patients with physical illness. Having completed her training in Ireland and England, she returned to Ireland and commenced a course in Ceramic Design. She intends to work as a ceramic artist.

John Rees, MRCPsych, is a Consultant Psychiatrist in Basingstoke, North Hampshire. He trained in Psychiatry in London and in the Wessex region. He has a particular interest in the teaching of psychiatry, in the management of psychiatric crises in general medical settings, and in the history of medicine.

Wilhelm Skogstad, MD (Munich), Psychiatrist (Munich), is Consultant Psychotherapist and Head of the Adult Unit at the Cassel Hospital, as well as a psychoanalytic psychotherapist in private practice. Having worked initially in general medicine, he then trained as a psychiatrist and psychoanalytic psychotherapist in Germany and, later, in the UK at the Tavistock Clinic and the Cassel Hospital. He is currently completing his training with the British Psycho-Analytical Society.

Foreword

I am pleased to have been asked to write an introduction to this book for I have long valued and respected the work described therein. This is an extremely painful book – it tells it exactly as it is in institutions. There is therefore, perhaps, a slight risk of evoking defences against psychic pain in the reader. I urge you to persist in reading it, for it gives an excellent picture of institutional psychic reality. Observation after observation spells out the despair, the misery and the pain of the patients and the reaction of staff who go about their daily tasks in this field 'irradiated' with distress. The present fashion in health management is much given to the creation of standards that are to be adhered to in the provision of services be they mental health or coronary care and for these standards to be monitored, audited, yea policed, to ensure compliance. I have little doubt that this will lead to some increased clarity of goals and some improved performance but I am old enough to remember the problems in cultures with centrist control and command structures and what a nonsense they made of genuine participation by the workers in the centrally set goals.

What in my view is crucially missing in this management approach is the underlying cause of why we have such management and morale problems in the NHS and such a gulf between front-line workers be they doctors, nurses and others in daily contact with patients and others who don't, managers, finance and the multitude of workers bombarding us with demands, circulars, newsletters etc.

What all workers, whether front-line or rearguard, are missing is what is so vividly described in this book. Chapter by chapter reveals the despair, the pain, the mental dulling mechanisms, the defences against pain that all are subject to. The front-line workers are too caught up in attempting to maintain their self and emotional survival to be able to reflect on what they are caught up in, the rearguard workers 'know' what is going on with a 'clarity of blindness' that comes from never going near the coalface of the workplace and further distancing themselves from the pain by engaging in the all too familiar game of 'them and us'. The beauty of the book is that it is rich in detail giving page on page of observation of what happens in various National Health Service settings. The majority understandably are of mental health or better said mental ill-health settings but there are enough descriptions of other everyday health services to give the book a wide application. It is only by taking into account the 'ecological baseline' of the NHS as described in these chapters that progress can be made in creating the much vaunted new NHS – modern, dependable, equitable.

The book does not set out to address issues of what might be done about the personal and institutional dilemmas so graphically described. It sets its task as presenting the reader with the 'facts', and leaves one to find one's own way of responding. The response could then range from the recognition of these phenomena in oneself and in one's institutions, to moving in the direction of management, or action research, or consultancy interventions such as have been pursued and recorded in the work of the Tavistock Institute, the Tavistock Clinic and other organisations.

The observation approach described in this book thus brings the possibility of *observation* leading to *intervention* one step nearer – supporting forms of practice and intervention characteristic of, for instance, the Cassel Hospital and the Tavistock Clinic.

In passing, it is interesting to note that there are several current 'models' of observation. The one described in this book is one in which observers study organisations that are like or similar to their own. The Tavistock Institutional model, by contrast, is one where students are encouraged to negotiate entry and observation to any institution that interests them, with a proviso that they should avoid observing the kind of institution that they, as part of their career-training or present work, are familiar with. The emphasis is therefore on developing a semi-detached, 'visiting anthropologist' in-yet-on-the-boundary state of mind. The Tavistock course has two aims – to enable workers to achieve a 'safer' personal perspective on the institutions they work in and on the other hand to have a detachment such as might be helpful in forming the foundations for institutional consultancy. The debate is as in this book – is it an advantage or a disadvantage to 'know' about the organization one observes or consults to – another variant of the ongoing clinical debate of whether one should or should not go into clinical assessment services 'free of preconception' or not and how this is to be achieved. There is certainly room for several models, and this book goes a long way to furthering the debate.

This is a much needed and welcome book that does 'tell the truth' about life and death in the health services in a most impressive and clear style – its application is international, its readership should be all concerned from politicians to managers to those in intimate clinical contact.

Anton Obholzer
January 2000

Preface

Generally, a preface tries to give the reader some sense of how the book began and evolved. The collaboration between the two of us originated in an asymmetry. One (RDH) started this work some 15 years ago, whilst the other (WS) has been involved for less than half that time, first as an observer and then as a colleague. It seemed interesting to explore the differences and similarities in our commitments to the collaboration between us.

RDH: I can go back to the days when I was first interested in psychiatry. At that time, there was a vigorous reaction against institutional psychiatry. In the 1960s, those institutions often appeared to be the cause of mental illness – not a means of containing it. I was struck by those large institutions and the insensitivity I found in the attitudes to mental patients in psychiatry.

WS: The experience of insensitivity may have been important for both of us. At the start of my medical career in Germany I worked on various speciality wards within internal medicine. My experience on some of these wards was that patients were often treated as a collection of organs rather than as suffering human beings. I found myself interested in the way patients experienced their illnesses as well as the emotional difficulties that may have contributed to their physical illness, but I felt very alone in this. This led me to go into a psychosomatic department and to start a psychotherapeutic training.

RDH: I, too, on entering psychiatry, found that there was a tendency to treat patients at arms length – an emotional arm's length. I remained puzzled and concerned about this when as a consultant psychotherapist I had a role in teaching psychiatric trainees. I became aware of a typical progress psychiatrists made during their training. Under the pressure of the work, the psychiatric culture and the career structure, their human responses to suffering patients often seemed to be progressively numbed. I had known many of the trainees as medical students and often felt that it was the most sensitive and humane of them who chose to become psychiatrists, but at the endpoint of their long journey of training they seemed to have become hardened. By then, many had learned to keep a cynical distance from their patients, or had a deep bitterness against the system in which they worked; and, unfortunately, often passed this on to their own trainees.

WS: The process you describe seems to have something to do with the pressure of the culture and the institutional dynamics. In the environment of medical wards I worked in when I started, I was intrigued by the difference in the way patients were treated on different wards, much more humanely and empathically on some and more distantly and mechanically on others. I had a dim sense that this couldn't just be to do with the particular people working on those wards, especially as I found myself being different to patients on one ward than on another. When I came to England, I got to know some of the psychoanalytic thinking about institutional dynamics. I also attended one of the Leicester Conferences, which gave me a vivid experience of the power of those dynamics one gets pulled into, and this suddenly made sense of some of my experiences in medical, psychiatric and psychotherapeutic institutions.

RDH: Well, the Leicester Conference experience was obviously formative for both of us. There, one somehow tries to make sense of what is happening under the surface, whilst being subjected to all those hidden pressures one is trying to identify. When I was at the Leicester Conference, I was impressed that one is somehow in the same position as a psychoanalyst – being put under various pressures from the patient, such as the transference, whilst trying to identify them.

WS: It is very difficult to do that, though, when one is part of an institution. When we met, at the Cassel Hospital, I valued your attempts to make sense of the dynamics within the hospital that I often felt overwhelmed by. Your observation method, however, introduces a greater distance from which to look at the dynamics of such institutions by simply observing them.

RDH: That's right. When I was thinking about the training experience of psychiatrists, my thoughts turned to my own psychoanalytic training. There I had been particularly inspired by the observation of a mother and baby from birth that I was required to do. That exercise carried no responsibility for the care of mother and infant, and yet one did experience other anxieties, just from being an inactive observer. Such an observation seemed to be an important training exercise in experiencing the pressures of the family milieu and developing an emotional sensitivity to it. I was therefore wondering whether similar observations could help trainee psychiatrists develop their sensitivity to their patients and wards – rather than to become hardened against them.

WS: Well perhaps there are many reasons for doing these observations. When I became interested in carrying out an observation myself, I was particularly interested that this might help me look at and think about the dynamics of the institution I was working in, and potentially also to learn to consult to troubled wards. I was also interested to go back to where I had started from and have a different look at the atmosphere of medical wards. Your interest, I think, was more of an oppositional one, psycho-therapy versus psychiatry.

RDH: You may have something of a point there, since I think I do see quite a strong opposition at an emotional as well as at an academic level, an opposition that is sustained by psychiatrists and psychotherapists. I think both sides hold quite divergent value systems. But, you know, what I discovered in fact was something quite different. My initial belief was that there might be something oppositional and subversive of general psy-chiatric training in my project, but this failed to be endorsed. After Flavia Donati did the first observation (Chapter 3), the development of interest amongst trainees in doing such observations was astonishing: for many years I regularly had trainees coming forward for this experience volun-tarily. I realised that psychiatrists in training remain sensitively enquiring people; they wanted to attune themselves more directly to the suffering that was under their noses, despite the cultural demands their training seemed to make. So maybe the 'hardening' process didn't go as deep as I had thought.

WS: We have stressed the role of human sensitivity in medical and psy-chiatric work, but I want to add something: that is, the role of thinking – not just having feelings. When I started an observation as part of this project, some six years ago, it was a fascinating experience – not just to observe the ward and what happened around me and in myself but at least as much to think afterwards in the seminar about what might be under-neath all that went on. And that process of thinking and making sense of what I had observed didn't stop there, it went further when I sat down to write a paper and again when I showed what I had written to others like Isobel Menzies who then helped me again to see things I hadn't seen up until then and have further thoughts.

RDH: I agree with that. There is more to the observation process than simply to have a set of feelings. It is important to reflect upon them, 'as opposed to discharging them like the patient', as Paula Heimann said. In some ways this thinking process is as active as giving drugs. Again it is so easy to make an opposition between the kind of thinking that we psycho-analysts support and the prescribing of more active treatments that psy-chiatrists rely upon, but probably both are 'active' interventions. Thought and reflection is nowadays seen as the core ingredient in a psychoanalytic treatment, but that role for thinking can also be transported outside the psychoanalytic setting – to one such as ours.

WS: An important part of the experience for me was also the process of writing a paper about it, in which your seminar was very helpful. That step from registering the pressures and atmospheres of a culture to clarifying and formalising one's reflections involves quite a process, even a struggle, as Judith Edwards (Chapter 6) described.

What fascinated me about editing this book was that I could then take another step by further reflecting on the papers of others (those who hadn't yet published their papers but were in the process of writing them) and helping them to develop and formulate their own thinking. Is this where you think the research dimension comes in?

RDH: Yes, I think there is a smooth transition from observational reflections to research findings. As psychiatry moved on during the course of my career there was an increasing demand on trainees to carry out research and publish papers. These were usually drug trials, but some were keen to publish their observational experiences. They felt that they had seen things in their wards that they had never imagined or only had a vague inkling of, and so thought that this was true research whose discoveries were well worth communicating.

And when I became more involved in higher training and worked with those specialising in psychotherapy, such as yourself or Mark Morris (Chapter 7), I was more strongly challenged to formulate clearly the ideas that I was intuitively working with in the supervision seminars. And I also needed to clarify in what way such a project does actually contribute as research to the understanding of health care institutions.

The editing of this book has involved a very considerable process of further clarification which you have continuously pushed us relentlessly towards.

WS: Well, our struggle has actually produced a result that we are both pleased with. Let's hope our readers will be too.

In producing this book we have had to combine a record of an educational intervention in the training of psychiatrists whilst also entering a more research-oriented set of attitudes where the effort is to grasp some specific and valid method in the human sciences, the science of human subjectivity. The reflective process that has been generated between us in producing this book, in confronting each other's ideas and in struggling with our rather different writing styles, has formed, however small, an institution in itself. As you, our readers, observe your own reactions to the way we have worked, you may have some access into the stresses that are involved in jointly producing a book, and how we have coped with or evaded them in a manner we are now more accustomed to understanding.

Bob Hinshelwood
Wilhelm Skogstad
January 2000

Acknowledgements

The following chapters have been published before and are reproduced here in an adapted form with permission by the publishers:

Chapter 3 from: F. Donati, 'A psychodynamic observer in a chronic psychiatric ward', *British Journal of Psychotherapy* 5, 3: 317–329.

Chapter 4 from: J. Rees, 'Psychotherapy training: food for thought', *International Journal of Therapeutic Communities* 8, 1: 47–56.

Chapter 5 from: M. Chiesa, 'At the border between institutionalisation and community psychiatry: psychodynamic observations of a hospital admission ward', *Free Associations* 4, 2: 241–263.

Chapter 8 from: W. Skogstad, 'Working in a world of bodies: defensive techniques on a medical ward – a psychoanalytical observation', *Psychoanalytic Psychotherapy* 11, 3: 221–241.

Chapter 10 from: N. Ramsay, 'Sitting close to death; observation on a palliative care unit', *Group Analysis* 28: 335–363.

Part I

General introduction

Chapter 1

The dynamics of health care institutions

R.D. Hinshelwood and Wilhelm Skogstad

This book is about an attempt to understand health care institutions through the eyes and mind of a participant observer. The approach adopted by the authors is based on psychoanalytic thinking and ideas, and has developed under the influence of the tradition of the Tavistock Clinic and the Tavistock Institute of Human Relations.

Various trends have developed there for applying psychoanalytic ideas outside the consulting room. In the 1940s Esther Bick pioneered infant observation (Bick 1964), and this is now a customary method used in the training of psychoanalysts, psychotherapists and child psychotherapists.

The Tavistock Institute, a branch that grew out of and later separated from the Tavistock Clinic (Trist and Murray 1990), then established a tradition of applying psychoanalytic ideas to commercial and government organisations. Increasingly they deployed those ideas within the context of an overall framework from systems theory (Rice 1963; Miller 1993). This conceptual complex is widely used in consultancy work with large and small industrial and other commercial companies, government organisations, small temporary conferences (the Group Relations Training Programme), and applied to society at large (Khaleelee and Miller 1985). This tradition now has a strong influence in this field of work (de Board 1978; Palmer 2000).

Obholzer and Roberts (1994) from the Clinic have produced a body of work, which we shall refer to later, that seeks to redress the balance and to give psychoanalytic ideas a greater part to play. Their work has been largely directed at particularly anxious institutions in the health and social service organisations.

The present book also deals with health and social service organisations, but more specifically we have reinforced the psychoanalytically oriented method further, and started from Bick's original observation method for the mother–infant organisation. Therefore, it harks back to the founding ideas of the Tavistock tradition (Trist [1950] 1990; Jaques 1953; Menzies [1959] 1988).

The adaptation of this method to the observation of large organisations which form the basis of the studies in this book, will be described in

Chapter 2. In this chapter we will give an outline of some of this tradition of work on institutions, and especially health care organisations.

SOCIAL DEFENCE SYSTEM

Fundamental to psychoanalysis is the anxiety–defence model according to which an individual has conscious and unconscious anxieties and conflicts which are dealt with by developing psychological defence mechanisms. This is first of all a model of individual psychology.

Broadening it to understand the functioning of groups, organisations and institutions in terms of anxiety and defence developed during the 1950s, when Jaques (1953) proposed that a social system can support the individual's own psychological defences. His core idea is that, unconsciously, individuals can use the social system to help defend themselves against their anxieties. Although it is the individuals who feel anxiety and operate defences, a defensiveness can also be locked into the social system. As a whole, the system then operates in a way that allows the individuals to avoid certain anxieties and conflicts, in particular those which the institution's primary task provokes (Menzies [1959] 1988). Individuals co-operate in shared aspects of the social system to support more rigid and primitive defence mechanisms in the individuals. These unconscious defence mechanisms are reflected in shared, socially required defensive attitudes and in particular ways in which the work is performed. The standard forms of practices which develop within an organisation for defensive purposes are referred to by Menzies ([1959] 1988) as 'defensive techniques'. Though the practices themselves are social and overt, what drives them is personal and unconscious and can only be inferred. This divergence between the individual's own system and the system of the organisation was first recognised by Trist ([1950] 1990), who sought ways of bridging conceptually between the social and the personal.

In any work enterprise, individuals will experience anxieties from various sources. Some will be work-specific anxieties and some individual-specific. In most organisations these tend to combine. Firstly, any work situation can cause work-specific anxiety – the work may be a dangerous activity such as digging coal, or guilt-inducing if it is work in a factory for weapons. This is a specific anxiety that is generated by the work and concerns everybody.

The particular kind of work also shapes and limits the cultural forms of defences, because the nature of the work influences what defences can be employed. The defensive techniques in the mental health professions are, therefore, quite different from, for example, those in prison staff (Hinshelwood 1993) on both counts – the work-specific anxiety and the selective effect of individual-specific anxiety.

Another, less psychoanalytic, way of looking at such differences is the concept of the socio-technical system which was developed by the Tavistock Institute (Trist *et al.* 1963). This concept implies that the practical requirements of the particular type of work on the particular raw material (the technical aspects) have a strong determining effect on how the social system (including its defensive attitudes) grows up.

This approach was worked out at the Tavistock Institute in consulting work with the manufacturing industry. When we come to health care organisations the work and therefore the technology are likely to be vastly different. Health care organisations operate upon persons and not upon the qualities and behaviour of material things. The interaction between care workers (people with particular sets of attitudes about their kind of work) and their 'raw material' of other persons (patients or clients also with attitudes towards this work) is more complex, subtle and subjective than the cultural attitudes of an industrial manufacturing enterprise. The scope for mutual impact between one set of attitudes and emotional experiences and the other is obviously great – and is missing from work with inanimate raw material.

However, secondly, individuals bring certain concerns, anxieties and conflicts that are specific to them. They may be drawn into particular work or particular organisations because their defences match aspects of the social defence system of an organisation (Dartington 1994; Roberts 1994b).

Of course, many other factors shape the working techniques. These will arise from economic, social and historical sources, but these are not the primary focus of this study.

HEALTH CARE INSTITUTIONS AS SOCIAL DEFENCE SYSTEMS

In the 1950s, Menzies carried out an extensive study of the nursing service of a general hospital, using an interview and questionnaire method. She described in detail how the social system was influenced to support psychological defences against the anxieties of the primary task (Menzies [1959] 1988).

Menzies' classic study is the reference point for most later psychoanalytically oriented work in health care organisations. She took a specific view of the anxiety that drove the defensive systems. There are deeply unconscious phantasies concerned with human aggression, and the damage done, in phantasy, by that aggression. She spoke of the unconscious level of those phantasies, and how the real existence of damaged and dying people in beds in hospital could seem to confirm those phantasies as real. This uses Freud's notion of the omnipotence of phantasy (1909) – the idea being that if the phantasies of aggression are unconscious it is very difficult for the person to test in reality, if they have actually done what they unconsciously think of doing. In the unconscious, to think is to have already done the deed. These phantasies then add to the real responsibility and guilt, leading to extreme and unrealistic anxiety. Caring for the extreme cases of people dying can then act to confirm that inward feeling of burdensome responsibility. As a further step the person is then driven to repair the phantastical damage and to restore the damaged person to full health.

The closeness to suffering and death in the nursing work, the intimate physical contact with patients, brings up various anxieties connected with the burden of responsibility for illness, suffering and death. Many features of the nursing service that Menzies studied seemed to be aimed at helping the individual to avoid the conscious experience of anxiety, guilt and uncertainty, and achieved this by eliminating situations, tasks and relationships that caused the anxieties. For example, nurses were frequently moved from ward to ward, and various tasks in the care of patients were broken up between a number of nurses, so that no emotional closeness could develop between nurses and their patients. The depersonalisation and detachment was accompanied by a denial of feelings in nurses or patients. The processes of splitting and projection were seen as central to understanding the defensive system. For example, conflicts inherent in the responsibility were avoided by attributing all irresponsible impulses to the junior nurses and strictness and harsh discipline to the seniors. The crucial significance for the dynamics of an institution is that such projective processes do not remain on the psychic level, but become a reality within the organisation 'since people act objectively on the roles assigned to them', as Menzies put it ([1959] 1988: 57) – what we would now call 'projective identification'.

Menzies showed that the defensive systems interfered with the ordinary way in which people might process all this: firstly, by ensuring that all these feelings remained unconscious and therefore were not available to be tested in the reality; secondly, by disrupting the relationship between patients and staff so that staff never follow through the care they offer. This also prevents them from mitigating the phantasised guilt and demand to repair.

The externalisation of conflicts through the projection of different aspects into different groups within an organisation, which Menzies showed, for example, in relation to responsibility, is a common factor in the dynamics of institutions. In this way, what could be an internal conflict becomes an external one instead; this reduces the anxiety in the individual but leads to tensions between different groups and, because of the polarisation resulting from projections, often prevents appropriate solutions to the task.

Such a spreading of conflicts inherent to the task was found by Bott (Bott 1976; Bott-Spillius 1990), who carried out an extensive study of a mental hospital in the 1960s, using an anthropological fieldwork method. She described the mental hospital as being at the centre of a number of conflicting aims and intentions:

- the need to keep under *control* the madness which relatives and society in general find too difficult to tolerate and want to get rid of into the institution;
- the need to provide *care* for people who are looking for retreat and respite from the intolerable difficulties of their lives; and
- the wish to offer *treatment*, and even cure, to patients suffering from illnesses.

These different aims are often incompatible and come into conflict with each other. Bott found in her study, however, that such conflicts were not expressed or even directly recognised by the staff of the hospital. Instead, the conflicting aspects were spread between patients, doctors, nurses, relatives and representatives of society and thus prevented from becoming a difficult and painful conscious tension within individual staff members (or patients).

Miller and Gwynne (1972), using an action research method in a study of institutions for the care of the severely physically handicapped, also found social defence systems that support the primitive defences of denial, splitting and projection to deal with the conflicts inherent in their task, although here the division developed between different institutions. On the one hand, they found homes with a liberal attitude where inmates were regarded as having full human potential and were put under considerable pressure to develop whatever skills they might have. Miller and Gwynne called this the 'horticultural model' and contrasted it with the 'warehousing model' of other homes with a more paternalistic attitude. In the latter, inmates were seen as deeply damaged, with little chance of achieving any human characteristics and in need of total care. Facing the severe damage that makes normal life impossible for these inmates, recognising their surviving skills and potentials, and assessing both aspects individually and repeatedly over time, would involve anxiety and pain for both patients and staff. These were avoided by splitting and division across a fracture line which then had the effect that separate yet complementary attitudes could not be brought together. For those who failed the expectations in the 'horticultural model' this polarisation meant a denial of their full damage and distress, and for many in the 'warehousing model' a denial of their potential, leading to unnecessarily restricted lives.

A similar dynamic was found by Roberts (1994a) in a hospital for severely impaired elderly people, results which derived from a consultation method. There, a division between wards for rehabilitation and others for continuing care without the aim of rehabilitation led to a strict divide between hopefulness and therapeutic zeal in the first and a hopeless, devalued attention to the physical care and safety of patients in the other.

These are just a few examples of the organisation of health care institutions into social defence systems. These social defence systems co-ordinate the individual defences in which, at the unconscious level, the individuals bury their anxieties and conflicts. An allegiance to these defences within a collective work setting has an impact on the individuals' personal sense of identity. The denial of aspects of themselves through splitting and projective identification is more than an individual mechanism, but becomes, in a collective setting, co-ordinated between the intra-psychic states to employ such defences jointly. Each person gives unconscious support to similar kinds of defences in others and thereby contributes to a strong harmonisation within different groups. The insertion of individual people into the social structure is, therefore, a two-way relationship.

For example, in a mental hospital the fear of being taken over by madness and violence as well as the individuals' reparative wishes towards their primary objects can be kept safely controlled by projection into others. But this is co-ordinated by a social defence system, in which madness is kept in patients and sanity in staff and rigid barriers are created to prevent contamination (Bott-Spillius 1990; Hinshelwood 1987a; Main 1975). This, however, leads to severe problems in restoring patients to a degree of health in which they can re-own some sane parts of themselves.

Alternatively, the fear of madness in each person may reach the level of a joint, though unconscious, assumption that any liveliness between people might result in madness (Hinshelwood 1987a), which results in a specific culture of deadness and dampening of any liveliness (see Chapters 3 and 4). This leads us to a different concept: that of culture and its underlying unconscious assumptions.

UNCONSCIOUS CULTURE

'Culture' is an elusive term, difficult to define and yet an important concept when thinking about the dynamic of an organisation. The notion of the 'culture' was introduced by Trist ([1950] 1990) and strongly influenced Menzies' ideas about roles and work techniques in the practice of an institution. Menzies Lyth saw culture linked with

> such things as attitudes and beliefs, patterns of relationships, traditions, the psycho-social context in which work is done and how people collaborate in doing it.
>
> (Menzies Lyth 1990: 466–467)

When Trist ([1950] 1990) introduced his concept of 'culture as a psycho-social process', he wanted to relate these external aspects, of roles and practices at work, to the internal states of mind of the individuals who take the roles and perform the practices. Attitudes and sets of beliefs are cultivated partly as rationalisations for the defensive techniques and the schismatic projections described above, and they form part of the specific culture of the organisation or one of its sub-groups.

Culture, Trist claims, bridges the psyche and the social; it refers to the structural and instrumental aspects of social life as well as reaching down to 'emotional phenomena at the deeper levels of the personality' ([1950] 1990: 540). It encompasses techniques such as rituals, skills, customs, systems of strategy and tactics, and many of these techniques may appear as defence mechanisms against anxiety, i.e. what Menzies ([1959] 1988) later called 'defensive techniques'. But it also includes 'cultural patterns', which Trist located within the person. Some of the latter relate more to the external world, such as knowledge, skill, language, beliefs, values, prejudices and social attitudes; others are primarily internal, such as internal objects in the psychoanalytic sense. While the features of an institutional culture are carried by the individual members, they cannot be reduced to individual psychology; they exist within the reality of the whole organisation. The individual, however, has his or her own objectives, conscious and uncon-scious, for taking part in it.

In our thinking, we have tried to clarify this by focusing on one specific relevant element of culture. That element is the set of *unconscious* assump-tions, attitudes and beliefs about the work task and how to perform it. To claim this as cultural, this set of mental objects must be collectively held within the team of staff and patients – or by some identifiable sub-group of them. This collectivisation leads to characteristic work practices, but also to less tangible phenomena which can be best described as the 'atmosphere' – or the 'emotional atmosphere'. Human beings tend to be very receptive to an 'atmosphere', and respond often unthinkingly but emotionally and unconsciously to it. Our focus is therefore on this collectively generated and sustained atmosphere into which people come.

Though many things belong to culture, a psychoanalytic view directs attention to those that are unconscious – the unspoken shared attitudes, the unacknowledged anxieties and conflicts, as well as the quality of the atmo-sphere and its unconscious aspects. The social defence system is thus, in Trist's sense, a psychosocial process – sets of cultural attitudes which reach down to the depths of the individual personalities. This adds a distinctly personal dimension to the more social foci of attention such as task, role, authority and leadership. Unconscious defences generate implicit sets of attitudes which therefore form a palpable aspect of culture. Despite being unconscious, those aspects are quite dominant and remain influential because they are not recognised and accounted for consciously.

ANXIETY AND THE MANAGEMENT SYSTEM

When Miller and Rice (1967) at the Tavistock Institute embraced a systems theory approach, there developed a particular emphasis on the system itself and on the processes of system maintenance, in line with the current stress on management in organisational studies. Through this shift, particular issues within an organisation that are linked with the management of the system, such as task, role, authority, leadership and boundary, have become major foci. Their function within a system and the distortions and contradictions of these aspects in an institution are particularly looked at. One reason for this shift may have been the demand on the Tavistock Institute for consultancy work whose aim was to bring about actual organisational change, and thus led to an emphasis on the leadership and authority which must sanction and support, if not initiate, change. This different emphasis has, however, had the effect that the anxieties and conflicts that drive the distortions may not have such a central place, and are sometimes regarded simply as a category of obstacles to change.

Consultancy has also been the method employed by a group at the Tavistock Clinic in looking at the problems of health care institutions and other human services (Obholzer and Roberts 1994). They too have tended to stress the importance of leadership and authority in the work, while to varying degrees addressing the underlying anxieties.

In the studies described in that Obholzer and Roberts compilation, the consultant works with the staff, usually in a single weekly or fortnightly staff group meeting, or a 'sensitivity group'. This approach is based largely on the idea that those who work with people need to be sensitised to the emotional atmosphere and to the subtle non-verbal communications of feelings in their clients. The foundation of the work is that there are specific reasons why people's access to their own emotional states of mind are hindered. These hindering factors are sought within the unconscious of the team members, assumed to be collectively shared.

This workable and successful paradigm is based on the idea that someone from outside the team will have a vantage point not affected by these unconscious blocks. However, the illustrating case studies in the Obholzer and Roberts work convey an inconsistent view of the source of the unconscious 'blockages'. There are competing assumptions about where the block comes from. One assumption, psychoanalytically based, is that a social defence system distorts work practices as a defence against unfaceable anxiety in the work. But another model, based on systems theory, assumes that difficulties derive 'from other problems in the institution' (1994: 164), from organisational change at a super-ordinate level, giving rise to confusion over the team's primary work task. This is not an unconscious problem but a different kind of unknowableness – the unknown organisation beyond the team.

The two models are not necessarily in conflict, but the illustrations point to a need to diagnose in each case the type of problem that needs change. The same problem may sometimes also be addressed from different angles.

To give an example: Roberts (1994b) describes the consultancy work with a residential unit for children who had been removed from their families for their own safety. The children were to be prepared for future family life, either in their original family or with adoptive parents. Under the emotional pressure of pity and guilt and their own internal needs, staff had, however, distorted their task to one of providing the children with 'ideal parenting', to substitute and recompense the children for what they had never had. This was a distortion of the task and, in effect, 'anti-task', as it prolonged the children's stay in an institution meant for transition only. While the approach based on systems theory addresses mainly the distortion of the task and helps to clarify and change it, the psychoanalytical approach would want to address staff's unexpressed feelings of guilt and the unconscious assumption within the culture that they can provide ideal parenting.

Alternatively, in the work with a hospital for severely impaired elderly people, mentioned above, Roberts (1994a) found rigid boundaries between the aspects of rehabilitating patients and those of keeping them alive and safe. This situation may be looked at in terms of these boundaries and how they could be made more permeable, or, alternatively, in terms of the projective mechanisms and the severe anxieties connected with treating the incurables. One model can, therefore, be complementary to the other.

ANXIETY AND CULTURE

Our focus on the culture is a different perspective than the one on the management system, one that avoids the tensions we described by restricting the conceptual framework to psychoanalytic ideas and their application to organisational cultures. We have the advantage, too, of being free of the operational necessity to bring about change. Our emphasis stresses the primary role of anxiety and the distortions it gives rise to. By focusing on the atmosphere, the beliefs and attitudes that make up the culture of an institution, we preserve Trist's view of a bridge between the organisation as a whole and the internal 'culture' of the individuals. Therefore, in applying the anxiety–defence model to the organisation rather than the individual, the proper model is one of *anxiety–culture–defence*.

Thus, whereas the key factor in the work on social defence systems has been that of the explicit and visible 'defensive techniques', we would tend to add to those techniques the idea of a more 'internal' dimension, an underlying phantasy, or a 'defensive myth' (Rosenberg 1970). This draws attention back to psychoanalytic exploration of 'unconscious phantasy' as crucial within the culture and as central to the experience of anxiety and defence.

We will now address the collective anxieties in these terms. The 'myths' that make up the 'unconscious' aspects of culture can be expressed as specific attitudes to the work. We have pointed out so far that the culture of an organisation is shaped in three different ways by anxieties and defences:

1   First of all, specific kinds of anxiety are connected with particular forms of work.
2   Secondly, the people drawn to particular professions and certain fields within them are usually people with certain kinds of personal anxieties and defence mechanisms, and this in itself has a strong influence on the culture.
3   Thirdly, there are very different ways of dealing with these general and personal anxieties within an organisation leading to different kinds of culture.

Looking separately at these different points now, we must bear in mind that they are obviously interconnected in many ways.

The anxieties of the task

The specific anxieties in different work settings are numerous. In this book, we restrict ourselves to health care and related settings. In the Menzies ([1959] 1988) study described earlier, the author pinpointed several anxieties specific to the work of *nurses in a general hospital*. The closeness to people who are suffering, dying or mutilated is taxing and stressful, particularly because it stirs up deep-seated fears about one's capacity to damage and doubts about one's ability to repair. The fear of death is ubiquitous and not just located in patients, becoming a particular burden if one also feels potentially responsible for the patient's death. The experience of responsibility can be crushing, stirring up anxiety and severe guilt. Close physical contact with patients may arouse disgust and revulsion, but also libidinal and erotic wishes, impulses which may be difficult to control and cause anxiety. Apart from socially acceptable feelings such as pity and compassion, nurse also experience resentment and hatred of the patients and their demands, and envy of the care patients receive; such feelings, being much less acceptable, cause considerable anxiety.

More specialised areas of medical care may provoke more specific anxieties. For instance, in a *maternity unit* the experience of birth is beset by fears for the mother's life as well as the baby's. It also stirs up in midwives, nurses and doctors unconscious infantile conflicts around Mother's feared or real pregnancies and the birth of siblings, and more adolescent conflicts such as women's fears about their own bodies. Envy of the woman's capacity to have a baby, jealousy towards the (often idealised) union of mother and infant, and envy and hostility towards the baby, even if only unconscious, arouse anxieties and guilt in staff and may interfere with the ability to work. These issues are especially difficult and conflictual on a special care unit for babies, studied by Cohn (1994) and Fletcher (1983).

Particularly important for the studies in the present book is the complex of fears and anxieties that shroud mental health work. The historic horrors felt in the face of 'insanity' have not vanished through its definition as 'mental illness' and modern knowledge about it. While physical illness can be seen as separate from the person's identity (something 'one has'), mental illness is experienced much more as part of, or catastrophically affecting, a person's identity. The destructiveness directed against thinking and integration that is part of mental illness is felt intensely by those around them, most of all the relatives but also the workers. The fragmentation and confusion in some of the patients can arouse enormous anxieties, not only in them but also in those close to them. As Bott-Spillius (1990) puts it, they feel that 'something absolutely crucial in themselves is being attacked' (p. 590) and that 'their minds are being damaged' (p. 604).

Mental health is, of course, dealing not only with madness but with the experiences of severe mental pain, of depression, severe anxiety and breakdown, of violence and self-destructiveness. These are experiences that are much closer to many of us than we would often like to believe, and anyone working with such patients will experience (consciously or unconsciously) the fear of being contaminated by such feelings and losing control over themself. Talking to patients and empathising with them can, therefore, be felt to be dangerous.

When one is looking after other human beings who suffer, whether from physical or mental illness, anxieties about one's competence and abilities easily become intense, particularly when burdensome responsibility is involved. In the caring profession, it is to a large degree the worker's self that is felt to be the major tool for benefiting the patient or client (Roberts 1994b). Therefore, workers are bound to feel vulnerable in their core selves and anxious about their achievements.

The list of anxieties mentioned here for different care contexts is not comprehensive and cannot be. Anxieties and conflicts are both legion and specific to the task and will be discovered uniquely in every case.

What the carers bring with them

It is, however, not just the specific anxieties and conflicts that the particular work involves. Different work also attracts different personalities, with specific anxieties, conflicts and defences, and these may be helpful for the work but may also hinder it and undermine the containment of the inherent anxieties (Dartington 1994; Roberts 1994b).

People in the helping profession frequently had the role of carer in their own family and this has become an indispensable part of their identity (Roberts 1994b). Moreover, they may be motivated by unconscious reparative wishes towards their 'primary objects', in particular their mother. Such wishes develop, according to psychoanalytic theory, out of a sense of guilt for one's destructive impulses. These reparative wishes may be important in helping one through taxing work, but the original feelings of guilt and anxiety about one's destructive impulses remain active and, if one cannot cure or repair with perfection, may come to the fore again. An important aspect of becoming a helper may be a deep-seated fear of helplessness and loss of control and an attraction to omnipotent expectations of one's capacity to cure. Even a sufficiently good performance may feel like a failure when measured against such omnipotent and narcissistic expectations, and feelings of helplessness, which are so often part and parcel of the work as a helper, may cause severe distress. Workers are then often driven to project their own feelings of helplessness into the patients, and any experience of helplessness may fuel resentment towards the patients who do not fulfil their workers' exaggerated expectations. Pent-up resentment may escalate, as these infantile phantasies are frustrated.

An interest in and empathy for, other people's distress and mental pain is essential for work in mental health. These are often rooted in one's own emotional development and the particular emotional difficulties one experienced. Such an interest may be based on an understanding of one's own mental pain and a capacity to tolerate emotional distress. However, often people, who deeply fear states of mental pain, such as anxiety, confusion, sadness or depression; are drawn to mental health and this fear may lead them to wish to keep painful states of mind under rigid control in others. They may then try to do this by taking on the role of sane nurses or doctors to the 'mad ones'. This, however, makes workers unable to help patients with their own disturbing feelings, as they can no longer empathise with their patients' states of mind which have become too dangerous. Instead they may resort to ever more violent projections leading to an escalation of treatment measures (into specialling, physical restraints, increased medication, ECT). By then these measures have lost their therapeutic value and have deteriorated into a means to keep at a distance and under control what is unbearable.

The third shaping influence of anxieties and defences on the culture is the collectivity of the individuals as they adjust or distort their work practices. These vary from organisation to organisation and with them the way anxiety is 'contained' within the culture.

Defensiveness versus containment

While both the task-specific and the more personal anxieties and conflicts colour the culture of an institution such as a hospital, we have pointed out that they may be dealt with in very different ways in different institutions. They may be sufficiently contained (Bion 1959) within the organisation by different aspects of its culture and by certain capacities, especially of the senior staff, or they may not be contained and then lead to a very defensive system. This distinction between a system that deals with the anxieties in an adaptive, helpful way and a rigidly defended system links in with Bion's (1961) notion of a 'work group', i.e. a group that functions on a mature level and deals adequately with the group's task, and a 'basic assumption group' which is under the sway of unconscious needs and anxieties.

Many of the observations in this book show how the cultural processes lead to considerable further anguish for staff, in addition to the anxieties of the primary task. Significant coercive pressure may be applied to get people to conform at unconscious levels. Menzies ([1959] 1988) described how this pressure can lead to interference in job satisfaction and a consequent demoralisation and serious attrition of staff. Obholzer (1994) finds a different formulation when he says that 'a style of work that is essentially and consistently defensive is bad not only for the work but also for individual workers' (p. 178).

On the other hand, of course, proper containment of the anxieties and conflicts that people within an institution face can affect positively the work done for patients or clients, and is also a positive good for the workers and their own job satisfaction. People are often dissatisfied and frustrated in institutions, but very often the reasons remain obscure, and what is bemoaned may have little or nothing to do with the deeper reasons for their frustration. For effective thinking about organisations, however, we need to understand the deeper roots of the problems we complain of.

CONCLUSION

The studies contained in this book emphasise the need to bridge the suffering in the work and the personal suffering of the staff. They may sometimes appear to overemphasise the effects of anxiety; perhaps that is inevitable with observational studies of this kind. These observations take place right at the interface between patients/clients and primary workers and therefore look at the people closest to the source of anxieties.

What we present in this book is a series of observations. They comprise an inwardness, a sense of understanding and a subjectifying of the field of observation (as opposed to the more conventional research paradigm of objectifying). The key element of psychoanalytic research is the foreground position of subjectivity. The psychoanalyst is an observer of his own sub- jective experiences in his setting as much as an observer of his patient's experiences. Much the same goes for an observational method for organ- isations. Each observation rests on the observer's subjective experience in the observed organisation as much as on their objective description of what they can observe. The observer observes his or her own subjective experience within the culture. In common parlance, they must pick up the 'atmosphere'. The atmosphere and its fluctuations are the dynamic process of the organisation.

In conclusion, to define our own stance, we have addressed the question: What is the subjective field of observation at the level of the organisation? And we have answered that it is the 'culture' – or certain crucial aspects of it. We have therefore worked with a third term inserted into the anxiety–defence model, giving us an anxiety–culture–defence model.

We will move on to describe in detail the method of observing an organisation in the next chapter.

Chapter 2

The method of observing organisations

R.D. Hinshelwood and Wilhelm Skogstad

We cannot approach organisations with the same research method as we employ in a psychoanalytic practice. When observing a complex organisation (usually part of a larger one), rather than an individual, we do not have the brief to treat and give interpretations, and so feedback on our conclusions is limited. In this respect our position is closer to researchers using psychoanalytic ideas than to those in a psychoanalytic clinical practice.

To explore how an organisation works at unconscious levels – both for a general theory and for a specific organisation – we need to consider the methodological approach. Psychoanalytically informed social psychology has employed a large number of methods: questionnaire and interviewing techniques, an anthropological fieldwork method, action research, and the results gleaned from commercial consultancy work.

However, psychoanalytic practice involves a very specific skill – that of the participant observer. In the clinical setting, a psychoanalytic participant observation has five aspects: a way of observing with 'evenly hovering attention' and without premature judgement; the careful employment of the observer's subjective experience (sharpened as much as possible by personal psychoanalysis); the capacity to reflect and think about the experience as a whole; the recognition of the unconscious dimension; and the formulation of interpretations which afford a means of verifying (or falsifying) the conclusions the psychoanalyst has arrived at through this process. While this last dimension, the interpretation, belongs only to the clinical setting, all the others can be transferred to psychoanalytic research outside the clinical setting.

One similar naturalistic research practice is fieldwork in sociology and anthropology. Hunt (1989) compared classical methods of fieldwork with one informed by psychoanalytic ideas. Most importantly, psychoanalytic contributions support those methodologies which recognise the object–subject relationship and oppose the positivist methods of observation. Heald *et al.* (1994) refer to some anthropologists (Devereux 1978; Lewis 1977) who have moved away from the classical attempt to reify a society in objective terms and take account of the subjectivity of the observer as well as the members of the culture under study. This approach comes near to a psychoanalytic framework, which demands introspection and observation of the observer him/herself. It acknowledges that much of the observer's experience occurs outside conscious awareness; it is influenced, sometimes deeply, by childhood experiences of the observer, and observations arouse intra-psychic conflicts which not only affect the observation but can be important indicators within the observation.

Our approach is clearly in line with this but derives from a method that is most closely akin to current practice of psychoanalysis – the method of infant observation (Bick 1964; Perez-Sanchez 1990; Miller *et al*. 1989; Reid 1997). There, a participant observer visits a mother and her baby and attends to their interactions regularly over a period of time, using his/her emotional reactions and the help of a seminar group for understanding. Pioneered by Bick, infant observation began as a training exercise for child psychotherapists at the Tavistock Clinic and later for psychoanalysts at the Institute of Psychoanalysis in London. The original intention was not a research one, but a training exercise in the method of psychoanalytic experiencing. Its aim was to enable potential psychotherapists and psycho-analysts to hone their intuitive sensitivity to human experiences and situ-ations and to begin to develop a psychoanalytic attitude in which one retains, feels and thinks about the experience of the other, the observed, without an immediate recourse to acting on the internal and external pressures.

This method of infant observation prompted the development of the method of observing organisations used in the studies of this book. In a similar vein to infant observation, this method arose mainly as a training exercise. The aim was to develop a sensitivity to the human dimension and culture of an institution and to the anxieties and pressures within it. Thereby it can also sharpen one's own sensitivity within the work role in the institution, and thus to give help in thinking about the pressures and pulls of the culture of the institution.

THE OBSERVATION PROJECT

One of us (RDH) established organisational observation as a training pro-ject for young doctors in psychiatric training.[1] The purpose was to enable trainees to develop their sensitivity to ward atmospheres and team morale in the psychiatric service, without the encumbrance of their organisational role and the barriers of the metaphorical 'white coat and stethoscope'. Invited to take off their white coats and to go onto the wards in a quite

1 The first observation conducted in this project was that reported in Chapter 3.

different role, in effect, restored to them the experience of being ordinary persons rather than just professionals.

The observations turned out to be successful in the sense that trainee psychiatrists became eager to join this course. They seemed to appreciate greatly the opportunity it afforded them to reflect on their work and their chosen career in a way not possible in the general training programme. They were at a stage in their careers when they were coming into psychiatry, and were often aware of the tensions in the psychiatric teams. Considerable change was occurring at the time, as psychiatry in Britain converted as best as it could from an institutional base in the old mental hospitals to community care. They were aware of the criticisms of the mental hospitals, and indeed the seemingly deadened atmosphere in many long-stay wards. They wondered why this occurred, and often felt strong sympathy for the inmates (and also the nurses) who seemed victims of the system, whatever it was.

The project was then extended to those training specifically to be psychotherapists in the NHS (many with a medical background, such as senior registrars, or specialist registrars in psychotherapy). An observation project of this kind was felt to be a useful training exercise for such people who would be making a career within care institutions of one kind or another. One of the important features of a consultant psychotherapist's job in the NHS has been described as offering understanding of the state of the psychiatric institution in which they work (Hinshelwood 1987a). The observation project was one setting to foster such understanding.

Although the main intention was for training, several of these observations resulted in formal papers accepted for publication in peer-reviewed journals. This book presents a selection of these observations, some of them already published in journals, and some appearing here for the first time. Because of the original purpose, the range of institutional settings is restricted to those within the mental health, general medicine and social services sector, but the method itself could equally be applied to other institutions.

As the project developed, supervision of the observations began to be organised in the form of a small seminar of 2–4 participants, with one of us (RDH) as seminar leader.[2] The observers remained in the seminar for a minimum of nine months, and the membership overlapped so that the seminar as a whole built up experience which could be passed to newcomers. The whole period within the seminar consisted of three phases.

In the first three months, the observer was expected to do a small amount of reading. The minimal requirement was Menzies ([1959] 1988), Miller and Gwynne (1972) and some of the papers completed by previous members of

2 Some of the observations reported in this book were therefore not conducted with a group supervision.

the seminar. Reading and participating in the seminar discussions helped to start thinking about institutional dynamics. During this first phase, the observer also negotiated with an organisation of their choice for permission to conduct an observation and was helped in this process by the seminar group.

In the second three months, the observer conducted the actual observations. These were done once a week, usually for an hour, for probably 12–13 observations. Whilst the observations were in progress, the observer wrote detailed process notes after the observation, and these were presented in weekly turns to the seminar and discussed within the group. During this phase the observer used the seminar to report back to for advice and support.

Then, in the final three months of attendance at the seminar, the observer would reflect on the observations, and commence the task of organising the mass of material. The suggested aim, which most observers have followed, was to write a formal paper. This was seen, first and foremost, as an exercise in organising complex material of a subjective kind which initially often felt overwhelming to the observer. Most but not all observers have written a draft paper, and, perhaps, half of them have worked further on it after leaving the seminar to produce a draft to submit for publication somewhere.

THE OBSERVER'S ROLE

The observer is an intruder into the organisation, and has no part in any formal procedure there. Sometimes, therefore, the negotiation to observe an organisation proves complex and in one instance during the course of our seminar actually failed to achieve permission. Approaching and entering the organisation and negotiating the project, however, is in itself an integral part of the observation. The reaction of the organisation, the web of authorities who often seem to be involved in granting permission, and the attitude of willingness, scepticism or fear are the first important, indicative experiences. One can already observe some of the functioning of the organisation as it deals with intrusion from the outside and with the idea of being scrutinised. Essential clues are also gained from one's own emotional responses to entering the institution and to being treated in a certain way. Therefore, this initial experience already gives a lot of important observation material.

The observer initially needs to identify, perhaps by telephoning the ward or unit or by speaking to someone they know in the wider organisation, the senior person in the organisation who can authorise the observation. The observer will then write formally to this person, and almost invariably a response is only gained after a follow-up phone-call. In most instances this results in an interview with the senior authority, but there may be both managers and clinicians with authority over the unit, and sometimes they will all need to be met. What is usually required is a brief explanation of the observation, its purpose and its expected results. This in itself causes anxiety in the observer, who is expected to explain a role s/he has so far never experienced. The personal training aim is always emphasised. A final report will usually be mentioned and reassurance over confidentiality is given. Usually one of those in authority then asked the team in the ward/unit to accept the observer, and eventually effected an introduction in some way. The observer again explained the project to a meeting of the team. This gives a first chance of listening in to the anxieties of the team that will be part of the observation. Where possible and necessary, reassurance is given about the proposed observation and any anxieties it arouses. Practical issues such as time, day and the most suitable position for observation also need to be negotiated at this stage.

During the three months of the observation proper, the observer visits the organisation once a week at the same time and sits for an hour in the chosen place. He/she should sit in a position which gives a field of view (and hearing) that is as wide as possible, though inevitably it will be restricted. The interaction with the people of the organisation is polite, a 'friendly reserve'. Inevitably the observer will notice and feel linked with some rather than others in the organisation, all of which is part of the observation to be noted.

Initially, as in Chapter 3, the observer changed the time and position of observation in order to achieve a wider scope of experiences of the organisation. However, in subsequent observations we modified this in order to create a consistency of the observation for the observer and for the organisation, too. The consistency helps the observer develop his/her role and attitude as observer. The brevity of the observation means that it can only glimpse the life of the ward through a keyhole. The observer and the seminar need to become reconciled to this limitation. It is assumed, however, that the culture, or atmosphere, though fluctuating somewhat in the day (and throughout the space), will tend towards a constant quality that can be sensed throughout.

A period of three months is considerably shorter than the period of an infant observation, which goes on for a year, at least, and sometimes two. However, infant observation has a developmental focus – how mother and baby evolve together in the first weeks, months and years of life. An organisation, in contrast, though constantly on the move, will, in its cultural aspects, only change over a very much longer time-scale. The aim of the observation is therefore a synchronic, snapshot description rather than a diachronic study over time.

The consistency and regularity of the visits are important also because this enhances the link between the observer and the organisation. Though that link is in an ordinary way much attenuated compared with the link between the observer and the mother and baby, nevertheless a familiarity grows up, even if with an apparently impersonal surface. The observer always attracts a number of expectations – perhaps as a critical figure, or a support, or evidence of the specialness of the unit, and so forth, and these are indicative of the culture, comparable to transference manifestations in a therapeutic relationship. And the observer, too, finds, especially when they come to leave, a surprisingly personal attachment.

The observer will adopt an attitude, as far as possible, of open interest in whatever is going on. There is no obligation to engage in any other way, and the degree of responsibility is very low. While the focus in infant observation is the relationship between mother and baby, the one in the organisation is a broad one. As we argued in Chapter 1, the equivalent here is the culture, the implicit way people relate to each other, how they perform the activities, and the way they seem to go about achieving particular objectives. Above all, the observer needs to get a sense of the atmosphere of the organisation gener-ally, as well as specifically on the day, and the emotional quality of the interactions observed. Moreover, s/he needs to gauge the unfolding experi-ences s/he is having as observer, witnessing the activities, the pull to join in or retreat from them, the feelings of approval or disapproval, of like and dislike and so on, that will fleetingly pass across his/her mind. In summary, the observer endeavours to keep an eye on three things: the objective events happening; the emotional atmosphere; and his/her own inner experiences, the whole area of what in the psychoanalytic setting would be called 'countertransference'. All these areas of observation together reflect the qualities that make up the 'culture' of the organisation.

The observer will often be invited more or less pressingly to interact with people: a cup of tea or some of the food that is being served may be offered; s/he may be asked to explain the project; to identify his/her name, back-ground profession or whatever; or to give authoritative opinion or advice. The role of the observer is then not to remain stonily silent but to deal with these approaches courteously, neither seeming to be needy, secretive nor over-defensive. In general it is always possible for the observer to avoid getting drawn too much into a conversation which distracts the observer's attention from the wider field of observation. And those approaches by the organisation can be subsequently thought about.

The observer's role, despite its relatively passive quality, is usually an anxious one. Indeed, it is so partly because it is passive. Restraint from accepting invitations to become more involved is stressful and threatens to make the observer seem a rejecting figure. When distressing things happen, or indeed when joyful or exciting events occur, the urge to become involved creates an internal struggle in the observer. The weekly seminar must acknowledge these tensions and contain them. It then functions as the observer's background base – a home – in contrast to the ward or team.

THE FUNCTION OF THE SEMINAR

The observers meet weekly in a small seminar of three or so with the seminar leader. The purpose is a multiple one and on each occasion needs adjusting to the particular pressures that the members bring. The seminar needs to

- stimulate and clarify some theoretical reading at the start of the project;
- support the observer's initial negotiations with the organisation;
- regularly hear and discuss process reports of observation sessions;
- and assist and advise on the 'digestion' of the observation material, and with the structuring of a final paper.

As in all workshop seminars of this kind, an atmosphere of acceptance and non-judgemental advice is ideal. However, as is also typical, some of the atmosphere of the seminar will also reveal particular anxieties of the observers, and at times replicate the emotional quality of the organisation that is being observed.

The observer writes up the record as soon after the observation session as possible. He/she will put down all that is recalled, and order it in the time sequence of the actual observation – so far as this can be done. It is to be understood that the recording is not going to be exhaustive, nor completely accurate in an objective sense. A video recording would achieve significantly greater accuracy. However, against this loss in these studies, there is a gain which outweighs the loss. The gain is that the observer's recall inserts certain links and emphases which have been picked out by him/her without conscious understanding, or apperception, of them. This under-life in the records (psychoanalytically we would call it the preconscious or even unconscious awareness) is important material for the seminar to work on. Through these unappreciated aspects of the observer's own work the seminar can help to sharpen his/her subjective experiences into a new instrument for understanding the human situation being faced.

In his/her written process records, but also in what might be added when presenting to the seminar and in the way that this is done, the observer presents an account of his/her own sensitivity. It is important for the seminar to acknowledge the observer's intuitive awareness, and also to help him/her become more conscious of what s/he has picked up intuitively but is often not aware of initially. Turns of phrase, particular emphases on certain events or people, particularly asides and often those proffered with a humour that seems to dismiss them, and so on, are very important to pick up on. The seminar leader's role is particularly important in this respect, in helping to find the clues for this kind of 'countertransference'. It is impelling for the observer's learning that s/he has made the record in which others see things s/he has not seen. The observer can then reflect and assess whether this feels true, and if it does, can only grant that it was s/he who spotted it, albeit without this being consciously registered.

Sensitivity and intuition are not markedly supported and enhanced in professional health care trainings, especially not in medical training. This is why such a training exercise can be so useful, but it also means that the observer has to accomplish a degree of 'unlearning'. In an ongoing seminar, this kind of non-judgemental easing of the observer into a more subjective observing position can become the role of other seminar members, who have themselves been through that psychic movement. Again and again, naïve observers have found themselves impressed and excited by how much they have retrieved of their experience in a setting which has often seemed in advance to be characterised by its dullness or deadness. The discovery of the humanness of even the most impersonal situations enlivens almost all observers, and creates an impetus to persist with the often anxiety-provoking work of observing.

This training function of the seminar is its core aim, and initially its only one. However, as we became aware that these observations were providing material and descriptions of hidden processes in the life of wards and units, we began to realise that the work was a true research activity in its own right. As a result, the perception of the seminar itself changed somewhat, even though the work undertaken in it remained similar. Research into the subjective areas of experiencing has always been criticised for its unreliability, which stems from the character of the observer, his/her selective recall and selective forgetting. This is true and is a weighty criticism, yet it must be put beside the fact that certain descriptions and discoveries cannot be made, in the human sciences, in any other way than subjectively. The seminar, with its focus on the observer's subjectivity, is to a degree a tool for honing that instrument. Because the colleagues in the group have been involved in similar work themselves, while also having more distance from the observation that is being discussed, they may spot apparent gaps or an overemphasis on certain features and may thus function as a kind of 'cross-bearing' for the observer's sensitivity. Thus, in this kind of subjective observational work, the seminar of colleagues is as much the research instrument as the observer.

The seminar must also help the observer in the task of digesting the experience. This can be begun in the latter part of the observer's attendance at the seminar. However, this process of digesting extends well after the end of the seminar, and some have taken literally years to complete a paper. The purpose of the course is that it should be a grounding in a form of enquiry that will persist into the future career of psychiatrists and psychotherapists in institutional settings.

The seminar needs to find a balance between a theoretical underpinning on one hand and an openness to experience and received impressions on the other. Theory can so easily impinge upon and strangle the openness to experience. At the same time no subjective descriptive study of this kind can occur without some preconception. This is well understood in other comparable forms of study in the human sciences. Rustin writes about this dialectic in connection with infant observation:

> Psychoanalytical observation methods, like those of the field anthropologist or ethnographic sociologist, require observers both to have in mind a range of conceptions and latent expectations, by which they can give coherence and shape to their experience, and to remain open-minded and receptive to the particular situations and events to which they are exposed. They cannot know in advance which of the conceptions of which they are already aware will turn out to have a useful application. Nor can they be sure that any of their preconceptions will fit. They may well be confronted with experiences that, initially at least, fall altogether outside the bounds of their ability to understand them. What this method requires of its practitioners is the ability to hold in mind a loose cluster of expectations and conceptions, while remaining open to the experiences of the observation as it develops. They also have to be prepared to respond to and think about new experiences, both of the families observed and of themselves, which may not easily or immediately relate to their preconceptions at all. This is not altogether different from the situation of field observers doing anthropology or sociology.
>
> (Rustin 1989: 57)

This account applies equally to the observation of organisations as to that of infants. The method of observing organisations is close to fieldwork in anthropology and sociology, whilst its psychoanalytic framework of concepts is shared with infant observation. Thus theoretical preconceptions are inevitable, and form a sort of spyglass, but at the same time it is an overriding concern in the seminars that theoretical considerations retreat in the face of experience. The research claims of this method of observation must be modest and take the form of descriptive work that gives rise to hypotheses for further work, and for understanding that is useful in the institutional practice of professional disciplines.

CONCLUSION

Having described the method of observing an organisation and gaining understanding and sensitivity with the help of a seminar group, there is the final question of how the learning from these projects can inform institutional practice. Most of the projects were conducted by professionals in training, looking at organisations that they will in the future be working in and often taking a leading position in. Just as the aim of infant observation is to provide an opportunity to develop an analytic attitude, observing an organisation can help develop that particular attitude towards an institution. Observing and thinking about an organisation may also sensitise one to the dynamics of the organisation one is working in and may help one to think about, rather than act upon, the pressures within the organisation. In other words, the learning gained as a participant observer in these projects may move, psychically, to inform one's position as a professional worker immersed in just these processes. One may move from being a participant observer to becoming an observing participant.

Part II

Observations in mental health care

Chapter 3

Madness and morale
A chronic psychiatric ward

Flavia Donati

INTRODUCTION

Some people are chronically psychotic, and some people have to nurse them chronically. This chapter seeks to identify some of the dynamic processes that develop and become embedded when a small group of male nurses has the task of caring over the years for a large group of psychotic men, residing together in a hospital ward.

The method employed for this (described in more detail in Chapter 2) was to obtain and study a small but steadily repeated sample of life on the ward, visiting regularly for one hour a week for three months, using direct observation and subjective impressions. My aim was to examine how the population of chronic patients (who reside there) and the nursing staff (present only for the periods of their shifts) structured their relationship. One focus in particular was on how nurses coped with anxieties inherent in their task, especially those about chronicity, and whether there were modes of defence, phantasies and self-images held in common.

It is not my purpose to explain the absence of female nurses, the nursing policies and hierarchy of the hospital and the workings of the total institution. These have been much discussed since Goffmann's *Asylums* (1961) was published (Rosenberg 1970; Bott 1976; Menzies [1959] 1988; Hinshelwood 1979; see also Chapter 1 in this book). In a classical study of nursing in a large general hospital, Menzies ([1959] 1988) has shown that the way the 'primary task', nursing the sick, is carried out is only partly determined by the actual nature of that task. Otherwise it is heavily governed by the need to subdue and even eliminate from consciousness the intense anxieties generated in nurses by patients and their diseases. This leads to traditions, rituals and modes of conduct that amount to socially shared, imposed but unconscious devices to keep anxiety contained and unrecognised. As such they are brittle and ineffective and, from the point of view of the primary task, without rational justification.

THE FIRST CONTACT

Having obtained the permission of the consultants of the ward for the study to be made, my first step was to write to the nursing staff asking to meet them to discuss the possibility of observing the life of their ward for a short period. After ten days I rang the ward asking if they were available to discuss my project. They answered affirmatively with a query about limitations imposed by an industrial dispute at the time.

I met the nursing staff during 'hand-over' time (1.00 p.m.) for one hour. No further meeting took place during the three months of my observation. My project was approved and the next appointment was to rediscuss the results of my observations if they wanted to.

I arrived at 1.00 p.m. in the staff room. The nurses asked me repeatedly if I wanted tea. I said 2–3 times 'No thanks, I have just had coffee.' They answered 'We drink tea here. We cannot afford coffee.' Finally I had to accept a cup of tea.

The charge nurse asked where I came from and anticipated my answer saying 'Are, you from Argentina?' It was during the war in the Falklands. I accepted the challenge saying 'I am an enemy then.' I said I came from Milan in Italy. Immediately he started to tell how on holiday in Italy, he and two women companions wearing very short trousers were stopped from visiting a church because their clothes were considered indecent by a priest. Then a staff nurse who had looked at me several times during this long story said 'Let's go back to your visit.'

I explained my intentions and my not being connected with the team involved in their ward. Then I asked about life on the ward. The charge nurse was the spokesman. He said there were no problems, boredom, nothing interesting happened. He described the mixed age group of patients: 'We even have a 92-year-old man here for many years. They are very chronic people.' The ward's task lies between that of a locked ward and an open acute ward. Sometimes there is pressure for beds. One consultant never comes, the other only when he needs a bed to relieve the acute ward. He conveyed vividly their combined view: they were on their own there, the subject of no outside input or interest except sometimes as a dump. When beds were scarce elsewhere in the hospital 'they try to dump patients on us'.

No rehabilitation ward is linked with this one. The type of patient living in the ward is relatively independent. 'This could be a hostel or a day hospital. They don't need to be in hospital. In the old days patients were strongly encouraged or forced into rehabilitation. Now they do what they want. But I don't think people over 60 should be rehabilitated. What can you do with a 60-year-old patient?'

During the non-stop talk I encouraged this self-disclosure with comments and questions. The charge nurse went on talking about himself. At one time, in another hospital, he had managed to organise a set of part-time jobs in the firms surrounding the hospital, so the patients were all working. The ward was empty and he was just available for any urgent supportive intervention requested by the firms. The consultant had given him free rein. Then the consultant had left and all this organisation collapsed. The nurse had finally left demoralised. He had never recovered. 'What is the point? The role of administration is bigger and bigger. They can decide what to do. Nurses have no role any more. Once they were everything for the patients; now there are OTs and social workers who decide what patients should do.'

I asked about physical problems in the ward. 'No, no problems. We haven't had a death for years now! They don't want to leave us. We look after them very well.' The meeting ended with a 'go-ahead' for my plans. Other nurses had been silent but listened closely all through the meeting. At the end they asked me if I was going to play snooker with them. I mumbled some answer to disengage myself.

I had been welcome and they had disclosed some of their key problems very quickly. The confession seemed to come from their fear that I might discover their impotence. They seemed to say 'We know we are emptied of our functions, now performed by other people (occupational therapists, social workers, administration). We are bored without achievement and progress. You will not discover our impotence, we already know it!' Anxiety about this impotence seemed to be eased through an open confession.

Their first reactions were as if I represented a threatening new stimulus for the ward (an unknown female observer in an all-male ward). They coped by making jokes about my being an Argentinian enemy invading their territory with potential conflict. The weapons were not easy to find, but I felt in spite of their willingness that I was a problem to cope with. Moreover the anxiety about the presence of a female observer in an all-male ward seemed highlighted by the story of the challenge to the religious establishment by the provocative clothes of the two tourists in Italy.

THE SETTING

The role of observer

The observation method is described in detail in Chapter 2. My activity as observer was to focus on interactions, events, words and movements expressed by staff and patients and afterwards to record these in note form. Unlike other observations described in this book, I observed at different times of the day, but the timing was planned well in advance. The majority of the sessions took place before and after lunch, three were during lunch, and one at the community meeting. The place in the ward from which I observed varied; mostly it was a corner next to the entrance.

My aim was to be a neutral observer and remain as little a participant as possible. This meant limiting my own interactions with both staff and patients, so far as I could, to minimal responses, to listening warmly so as to provoke neither rejection nor feelings of being merely watched and judged. I was never formally introduced to the patients so they were at liberty to ignore me, address me, or find out about me. They were free to want or not want to relate to me, to know who I was or what I was doing there.

I would arrive at the fixed time, say 'Hello' to staff and patients, sit comfortably in any armchair and 'be there' for an hour.

The ward and its population

The ward was on the ground floor, shaped like a Greek cross, and was the only access corridor to and from the hospital's locked ward. The horizontal limbs were a dormitory, toilets and bathrooms. The vertical limbs were divided into three parts: the refectory next to the locked ward, a snooker and sitting area, and a TV and sitting area. The armchairs in the snooker area were arranged in one row facing the snooker table. In the TV area the armchairs were in two opposite rows facing each other. There was no private corner. The arrangements were all linear and square; more informal round ones were absent. Some posters hung on the wall opposite the windows, depicting distant scenes, two rhinoceroses, two boats on a river, two Thai girls next to towers, a square.

There were about twenty male patients; their ages ranged from 40–92 years and their length of stay varied between 10 and 60 years. All patients were autonomous in their daily routines; none were incontinent, nor with evidence of physical impairment (except for one blind and non-mobile patient, two severely physically impaired Parkinsonian patients and one with a neurological disorder). They all wore their own clothes.

The staff consisted of two daytime shifts of nurses (all male). The two charge nurses were British; all but one of the other nurses were non-British. One charge nurse and the non-British nurses wore white coats.

THE OBSERVATIONS

First session

In my first observation I found of particular interest how the interactions developed.

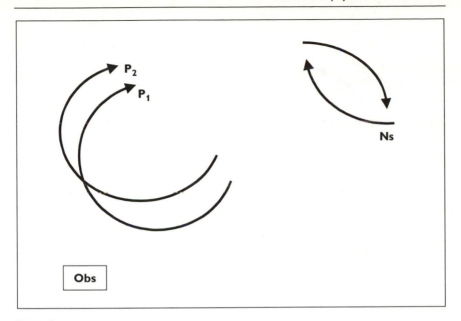

Figure 1

Initially the patients were all sitting in the armchairs, except for two who were moving around and who made contact with me. They commented about news in the paper and showed me a picture of a baby horse kissed by a woman. 'What do you like in it?' I asked. 'The baby horse' was the reply. The staff had warned me at the beginning about possible friction provoked by a wife of a newly admitted patient complaining about his management in the hospital. The nurses were moving around, further away from my place, sometimes making comments about problems in the ward and making little contact with patients (Figure 1).

After the first ten minutes, the charge nurse approached me and then stayed next to me on and off until the end of that session. The other nurses started to move around giving advice to patients such as: 'Comb your hair', 'Go for a walk', 'Why don't you go to OT' (Figure 2).

Some patients made brief contact with me. One of them talked to me about an actress (of my own nationality). Another patient offered me some of his home-made cake, made by his mother. The charge nurse, still next to me, protested that he hadn't been offered a slice. The nurses were still around but having little contact with the patients. Later in the session, the patients who had approached me were either sitting in front of the TV, walking around or going in and out of their rooms. Eventually, all the staff were gathered around me talking about their difficulties, similar to the situation in the introductory meeting (Figure 3).

During the observation I was addressed as madam, never as a doctor, and some compliments referring to me, exchanged loudly between staff, had

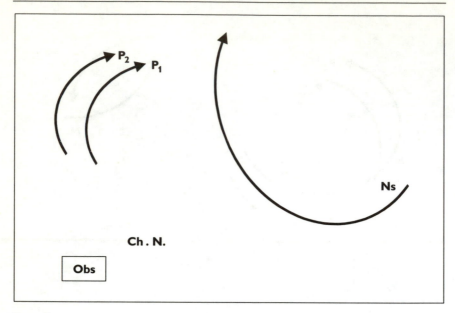

Figure 2

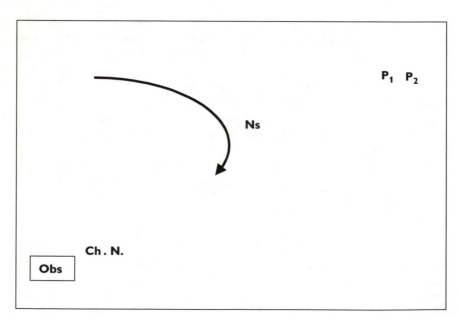

Figure 3

punctuated the time I spent there. On my way out, a member of staff followed me, saying in a manly and ambiguous manner, 'If you come after 9.00 p.m. I can tell you some secrets about the place.' I felt embarrassed, trying to stammer an answer.

Was I less threatening if seen as a female visitor, object of masculine comments, instead of being seen as a doctor visiting their ward with the possible view of discovering its life?

I left feeling surprised about the unexpectedly rich material and emotional experience observed during the hour, and at the same time worried and guilty. I wondered if I would be absorbed by the staff and kept away from the patients. Would I learn to accept the situation as an object of study, and not react to the discomfort of seeing the patients being cut off? Could it just be a tool for understanding?

Sixth session

Later on I observed the same pattern that I have described several times. Here is an example from the sixth session.

Entering the ward, I decided to sit next to a patient who was speaking loudly. No nurses were around. Soon after, a nurse appeared and asked if I wanted a cup of tea. I said 'No thanks, I am all right' and then he sat opposite me with a magazine. The patient asked him if I was his girlfriend. The nurse answered 'I wonder who is the lucky man' as if it was a conversation between men about an absent woman.

The patient asked three different questions of the nurse: about the nurse's exams; about the nurse's industrial action; and about ward matters. The nurse gave three monosyllabic answers and then started to talk only to me. The nurse moved from enquiry about my study project to describing how very bored he was with the ward's life, how difficult if not impossible it was to capture the patients' interest and promote interaction. Some patients were sitting around us and appeared to be listening.

The nurse was talking about the patients in negative terms with them around as if they were not there, as if they were not alive people who were listening, feeling and responding.

Now silent, the patient who had been speaking loudly stood up and went to sit somewhere else, then came back while the nurse was still talking to me (I was just listening). He sat for a few moments, then left again, sitting somewhere else and talking loudly to nobody. He seemed openly to express his discomfort at being cut off and talked about. His reaction did not change the nurse's behaviour. After a while the nurse was called by a colleague and left. I was alone looking around. The afternoon tea trolley arrived. A patient was serving the cups to a queue of patients and to those sitting in the armchairs. When it was my turn I was offered a cup of tea with biscuits as if I was one of them.

THE PHANTASY LIFE OF THE WARD

Depersonalised stereotype

I was received by the patients without question as to who I was and what I was doing there with them (they hadn't yet asked). Beneath the superficial impression of being accepted lay doubt about the real degree of personal contact. I was put, after all, in the same position as the patients and the general quality of the relationship seemed more of a depersonalised and stereotyped kind.

The nurses came back and went on chatting to me about 'how much better the female chronic wards are since women are capable of making wards their home, they are always doing something, looking after themselves and their environment. The atmosphere is much more alive, cleaner . . . more at home. Male patients neglect themselves, need continuous encouragement, the place is boring and the nurses alone have to try to make the ward like a home.'

The absent mother

I became the recipient of unceasing complaints, which were particularly painful when they were about the absence of some ideally warm environment that women make.

The work of the nurse in a chronic setting was a daily experience of giving care while getting little in return to show for it. The nurse's effort leads to no development, hardly any visible change, scanty appreciative response even of a rudimentary kind. Inevitably he will doubt the quality of what he provides and indeed the experience of any resources within himself. His identification as a nurse through the values acquired in his training and their validation by beneficial results with nursing care is enfeebled by the changeless quality of caring for chronic patients.

Everything bad was ascribed to the patients and seen as coming from them. They were regarded as empty, unmotivated, without wishes and drives, ungiving, unable to make the environment a regenerating, feeding, comforting one. The experienced emptiness seemed to be projected onto the patients in a clear-cut manoeuvre which left the nurse's own feelings denied and obliterated: 'Men cannot make a home.' Patients cannot make a warm home for both patients and nurses, but also the nurses are men, kept starving of nourishment and unable to provide for their patients: 'We cannot function as women, our breasts are not nourishing, we are sterile and impotent.' This seems to be the secret as expressed through the phantasy of a feeding and mothering environment elsewhere.

The absent supportive father

These feelings were aggravated by the sense of the ward receiving no nourishment from without, expressed so clearly by the charge nurse at my initial meeting with the staff. They had to feed but without being fed, female nurses and medical male technology and all maternal and paternal good things going elsewhere. No support received. No third party containing the anxieties in the carer/cared-for couple (father in the mother-and-baby couple).

Phantasies about the sterility of man-to-man relationships followed, although not openly in the clinical material.

Interpersonal contacts

Throughout the sessions while I was just sitting in an armchair, looking around, my contact with patients was largely restricted to exchanges of smiles and looks. The patients very rarely spoke to others; this was not because of gross cognitive impairment as there were some who could play cards, chess, draughts, snooker extremely well, frequently beating the nurses!

Both patients and staff would break this isolation in two ways: (a) on their way in or out of the ward ('Is it time for OT?', 'How was the walk?', 'Why don't you go out for a coffee?', 'How are you feeling today?'); and (b) in brief comments to the various passers-by who were captured momentarily with a challenging, appreciative or jokey comment from patients who were sitting in the armchairs as if waiting for something to happen. This *touch and go* behaviour involved everybody. This included the priest, whose two visits to the ward, while I was there, may now be mentioned.

On the first occasion he spent some time in close conversation with the staff, very much amused and laughing loudly about the stories I couldn't hear but which provoked some envy in me for the fun they seemed to have. Patients were watching silently.

His second visit was concerned with the slight, if not absent, growth in his potted plant which he had apparently donated to the ward. He discussed the matter with the staff 'Does it need extra care? Should I increase the watering?'

The priest seemed to fit in with the habitual exclusion of the patients and not to be concerned about the effect of his visits on the patients. Was I the only one envious of the exclusiveness of their fun? The priest was concerned about the growth of his baby flower: women's attention, efforts, might have been successful with it at least! The picture of the baby horse kissed by a woman, which a patient had shown me on my first visit, came back to my mind with his longing for a primitive relationship where care and tenderness produce nurture.

I have illustrated how the patients made feeble attempts but failed to make contact with me (first and sixth sessions), and how staff responded to this. On two other occasions they tried again; the first involved a patient who usually walked up and down:

'Are you Dr V's secretary?' – 'Why?' – 'Just to know' – 'Do you need to see her?' – 'Not really' . . . 'What nationality are you?' – 'Have a guess' – 'Welsh?' – 'No, have another one' – 'No, I give up.' When he came back again, he insisted on knowing my nationality. He then said a few words in Italian so I asked: 'Have you been to Italy?' – 'Yes, during the war' – 'As our rescuer?' – 'I don't know about that . . .' and he left.

This seemed another example of the *touch and go* behaviour and the difficulty of establishing genuine and deeper relationships, which will be explained later on.

During that day the whole atmosphere was excited, seemingly, as I discovered later on enquiring about the change, because the whole ward had followed the troubles provoked and experienced by one of their fellow in-patients who had disappeared and then reappeared with police. Agitation and excitement had spread round the ward.

The second time was of more massive proportion and I give the whole session (the tenth).

Tenth session

As soon as I arrived at 11.30 a.m. a patient asked a nurse, 'Who is she? A psychologist? – a doctor, a nurse?' The nurse gave an oblique answer like 'She is a friend of ours' and went on to me: 'Here is somebody who has been waiting to see you.'

An extremely large man walked towards me with a wide smile. At first I couldn't decide if he was a patient or a member of staff. 'He is Greek and wants to know you.' The nurse added 'His name is Angelo' ('angel' from the Greek angelos *– messenger). Angelo shook my hand, engaged me in conversation about my country, its wines, its beauties, and then offered me a cup of tea which I really didn't want and said so. He then nodded and left. Two patients passed by, talking about past financial difficulties. Angelo reappeared with a cup of tea for me. I couldn't resist! 'Milk? – 'Yes, thanks.' I smiled, defeated by the forced gift.*

Forced feeding

This was the first of his several forced feeding moves towards me and the patients. He wanted repeatedly to feed me with coffee, milk, biscuits, fried chips, etc. Although I tried to convince him that I wasn't hungry he wouldn't believe me. Perhaps he had projected onto me his own sense of deprivation in the ward starved of life, and was defending himself against the loss of his nursing role. He was feeling I was hungry, thirsty and was impelled to feed me.

Angelo then started to go up and down the ward making comments to sitting patients, particularly to Brian. 'Come on, take some steps, come towards me.' Half immobilised, carrying a catheter, Brian accepted the challenge and started to leave his armchair, trying out some steps, leaning on his walking aid. The patients looked at him as if he were something of a miracle. Brian was excited, talkative, laughing. Three patients came back from OT. Angelo welcomed them and they had a chat when Brian reached the corridor. Angelo had been called to the 'phone and was talking and laughing loudly. When Angelo emerged from the nurses' office he spent some time with Brian in front of a panel of pictures – photos – exchanging comments and laughter.

Angelo was very active and outgoing, walking around as if injecting life and energy into the ward. He was in charge of the ward just for that day in a shift together with another ward nurse (the other regular staff being absent), but he seemed to be immediately in touch with the needy, apathetic, emptied part of the patients and with the anxiety of being a nurse to them. Busily and cheerfully he seemed to deny the reality of the place and reminded me of the ephemeral light of mayfly.

Angelo asked loudly 'When is dinner time?' Somebody answered 'It is nearly time', and the trolley arrived. All but one patient moved to the dining room; he was feeling sick and said to me 'I can't eat the food here.' Angelo tried to convince him but soon he gave up. I was invited to join him and I sat, after they were all settled, on a chair next to the entrance of the dining room. Angelo was dishing out the meal with another nurse.

A patient, Brian, asked who I was. Angelo answered 'A friend of mine.' Brian: 'No – she came here before, a couple of times when my parents were here' (and then to me): 'Where do you come from?' I answered: 'From Italy.' Brian said: 'You are not Italian, are you?' I asked why I couldn't be Italian. He just confirmed I couldn't be.

Angelo was next to me and came several times to offer a potato or something else. I wasn't hungry, but a couple of times I was force-fed by Angelo. He even wanted me to take away a handful of chips in paper saying that I had to take it because he was eating and he'd feel guilty to be alone in this.

The other nurse in a white coat, before the start of the lunch, was very demoralised: 'There is such a waste in this place. Every day a lot of food is thrown away! You will see', he said to me. After a while he returned and was quite disappointed when he said 'It seems today that nothing will be left!' They were eating with unusually good appetites, at a more noisy meal than usual.

He had looked forward to having a witness for the waste (of the food and of his own energy, or life left behind, or skill . . .) but he could only show a little mashed potato. Another wasted chance.

The same patient, Brian, asked who I was and answered himself 'You come here to analyse our minds. We are nutcases.'
Another patient took me into his room to see a poster on the wall; it was the girl of his dreams. 'I am going to Copenhagen, I'll marry her and I will have the honeymoon in Denmark.' When after a while we returned to the dining room he came back and asked me to read some poetry for him – choosing one written by a woman – they were poems written by psychiatric patients. I read what he had asked and then he left, making some comments about the beauty of the book.
The session ended with some more offers of food by Angelo and some more verbal contacts initiated by patients.

I was struck by the number of contacts made. The ward's own staff were not there and their presence had been erratic for some days, and the new nurse somehow changed things by his general attitude, breaching their normal habits and the routine roles as old as the patients' stay in the hospital. The variety of the patients' contacts with me was very significant and powerful, now that I had been left available to them, and the general mood was elation (wanting to categorise me, 'Who are you', sharing their dreams, reading out of a book as if to a small child).

Individual personalities

Another issue emerged: how staff and patients deal with the recognition, expression, and encouragement of the individuality hidden behind the role of a chronic in-patient.

Once, in the eighth session, the charge nurse sat next to me and said 'Patients have their own routine, everyone has a different personality which should be respected. The one who likes to talk and the one who wants to be left alone . . . The nurses have an attitude I strongly disagree with. As soon as a patient becomes angry, restless, or different from his usual mood, they ask for new or extra medications. For me it is a sign that they still have some life.'

Personality differences were recognised but categorised by opposites. The third session showed how the problem of individuality emerged and found solution, at lunch time for example:

At 12 o'clock sharp the dining room was full, the music very noisy. The charge nurse dished out the meal. A staff nurse took it to the patients. The patients mostly ate without exchanging words. They were distributed at the tables according to their different 'types'. One was the table of the overeaters (obese-diabetics) who 'needed to be checked and who should not eat from each other's plates'. Another was the table of the poor eaters. At a single table a blind patient had the food placed in front of him. The other two tables were occupied by mixed, more balanced personalities.

This organised sub-grouping prompts some questions. What is this need for order, control and management in a setting where the staff complained about boredom, lack of initiative and co-operation among the patients and about their draining dependency? How are unexpected happenings viewed? Do the staff promote activity, co-operation, personal initiative in the patients?

It seemed to me that, in response to the experience of failure and impotence in nursing chronic patients, there arises a defensive urge to extinguish any sign of spontaneity, involvement, emotionality and expectations and to keep everything lifeless and predictable so as to avert new hopes, new disappointments and intensified frustration.

Ward meeting

Here there was another example of that from the community meeting held fortnightly in the ward, just restarted after three years, around the time of my first contact with the ward staff.

The charge nurse was chairman.

Ch: *'Who wants to say something?'*
Silence.
P1: *'Shall I be able to go home and work?'*
Ch: *'This question has to be put to doctors. Not to be asked here.'*
Silence.
Ch: *'How was the trip yesterday?'*
P2: *'Okay, that's all.'*
Ch: *'Steven, you wanted to organise a party. Why are you not saying anything now?'*
P2: *'Yes, a party . . . What more should I say?'*
Ch: *'Eh. Arthur, say something.'*

Arthur: 'I can't get my breath.'
Ch: 'Why?'
Arthur: 'I don't know.'
Ch: 'There is a suggestion to plan a trip.'
Silence returned.
P3: 'I want to see a social worker for a hostel.'
Ch: 'There are no hostels for you.'
Silence.
P4: 'I want to be transferred somewhere else. People here are stuck up.'
Ch: 'Are you happy here, Phillip, after so many years? Have you problems in communicating with people?'
Phillip: 'No.'
Ch: 'You see (P4) what is the problem? You never like where you are.'
[etc, etc, etc.]

The chairman seemed desperate to promote the patients' participation, but as soon as a patient brought up a serious problem it was either a doctor's matter or without viable solutions. Complaints, whatever the nature, however realistic they might have been, were instantly disproved and dismissed. Patients' expectations or beliefs were always wrong. The chance of a concerted group request was carefully avoided and the only attempt to elicit group opinions related to excursions.

In this material there were indications of an anxiety to subdue non-compliant thoughts on the part of the patients, especially the expression of desperation and impossible hopes. In line with this, the chairman (charge nurse) said to me after the meeting:

'It is hopeless. No response. We may as well not have these meetings. Patients always say the same thing every time.'

SOME FINAL COMMENTS AND SUGGESTIONS

My observations identified in the staff the use of inappropriate defensive manoeuvres against an intense anxiety.

The *anxiety* seemed related to:

- fear of constantly experiencing impotence and its confirmation in reality;
- an atrophy of professional skills;
- the uncertain identity and self-esteem of the male nurse role;
- and the stabilised 'madness' of their patients.

The *defensive manoeuvres* seemed:

- to maintain stereotyped and depersonalised relationships with 'touch and go' contact only;
- to reject the projection of the patients' feelings of despair, depression and hopelessness and to project all the failure onto the patients, who are constantly reminded of it. This reminding channels part of the aggression experienced in that frustrating relationship. The staff's poor self-image is projected and merged with that of the patients;
- to extinguish any sign of spontaneous involvement, emotional arousal and expectations, and to keep everything lifeless and predictable under 'efficient control'. The inhibition of new demands, or any chance of change or progress, contributed to keep the situation immobile, hopeless, lifeless and chronically 'mad'. It was a defensive manoeuvre that heightened the very threat it was meant to overcome.

There is a *self-perpetuating cycle* in all this: Threat (of impotence, loss of identity and skills, fear of outbreak of mad, sexual or aggressive excitement) arouses anxiety, leading to ineffective defensive manoeuvres which increase the threat and thereby the anxiety. The staff were clearly aware of the dissatisfaction of the patients but didn't seem aware of the self-defeating character of their defensive response.

Staff in such a predicament would need support through a reasoning and containing function like that of a father in the mother–baby couple. The *aim* of working with the staff in similar conditions should be:

- to help them in their self-observation;
- to explore sources of shared and deep anxieties;
- to establish more helpful defences; and
- to promote more genuinely personal interactions.

Chapter 4

Food for thought

The canteen of a mental hospital

John Rees

INTRODUCTION

It has been noted that too few people working in hospitals understand the experience of patienthood and illness. They shape their work as though insensitive to its impact – as if the disorder in their patients were somehow catching (Rosenhan 1973). Such attitudes are often attributed by hospital staff to society at large, but it is likely that these feelings are more generalised and that an exquisite ambivalence exists for staff themselves in their relations with patients, caring being only one part of their total attitude. It has also been noted that a result of the hierarchical organisation of staff is to reduce the amount of patient contact for those at the upper end (Stanton and Schwartz 1954). This can be very true for medical staff, since patients' requests for consultation may have to pass the filtering mechanisms of staff more intimately involved with them.

Such a gulf between the patient's and the attendant's experiences of each other is conceptualised in the notions of disease and illness (Helman 1981). 'Disease' is a pathological entity within the medical model of ill health, whereas 'illness' is the patient's perspective on his/her ill health based on psychosocial attitudes very different from the disease model. The clinical significance of this is that if medical care is to be most effective and acceptable it should treat both disease and illness. If not, poor doctor–patient relationships, dissatisfaction and non-compliance can easily result.

Medical training and practice (including that of psychiatrists) largely focus on the disease model and eschew any venture outside this. Psychotherapeutic thought, however, has long been interested in the doctor–patient relationship. To bring the psychiatric trainee into contact with some of these issues, trainees have occasionally been encouraged to undertake an observational study of some aspect of hospital life (Hinshelwood 1989; Chapter 2 of this book). This involves a considerable change in working technique, spending time with patients in a way very different from usual practice. At first this can be disabling; the protection and security afforded by the role of doctor has gone. However, the new information that can be obtained, and the management of anxiety provoked in such circumstances, can be very instructive when considering one's working practice with patients.

The hospital in which this study was undertaken is a traditional, large, psychiatric hospital, and, like many others, has experienced much in the way of change. The canteen was selected for observation, possibly due to a personal gastronomic bias. However, feeding is often interpreted as a basic way of expressing care, therefore how this function is performed and accepted may have important implications for the attitudes and practices of the profession and of the hospital.

The patient group was quite varied. A large number came from the admission wards, those who were felt to be 'well' enough to need little supervision. Of the more chronic patients there were those from rehabilitation and some from long-stay wards. There were also a fair number of patients who attended the hospital occupational therapy and works departments. Added to this were a few ex-patients and homeless persons looking for a free meal, with some success.

The nursing staff attending the canteen were drawn from a number of wards around the hospital. They were predominantly junior, mostly student, nurses in general training, seconded to the hospital for their psychiatric experience. The canteen staff were regular and did not spend time in the staff canteen.

The actual building was rectangular and relatively small. There were entrances in two corners. One was the main entrance; the other, leading to a ward, was used by the people from that ward but was locked much of the time. Many who used the ward door were able to get to the front of the queue which always developed.

INITIAL IMPRESSIONS

It has been remarked that a method by which staff stay in contact with their patients, but leave them emotionally, is to adopt some form of routinisation (Bott 1976) – concentrating on the organisation of activities rather than on the people who do them. Such routinised patterns lead to an 'authoritarian regime', and Bott noted a strong undercurrent of tension and fear associated with this. Her description was of chronic, long-stay wards, but it very aptly applies also to the atmosphere of the canteen.

When, prior to the study, I visited the canteen

I was unable to get into the dining area. A long queue came out of the entrance into a smaller waiting area, and was often so large that it curled in on itself many times. Nurses stood near the door, just inside the dining area, making the access rather narrow. I was unable to ask to get through and sat meekly on a window-sill instead. I rationalised this by thinking that the nurses would not want a doctor 'poking his nose' into how they ran the canteen, although in fact most would not be able to recognise me.

In reality it felt too threatening to approach. In discussion with my supervisor it was some time before I admitted that I had not been into the canteen at all, feeling rather foolish about this. After I started attending regularly, although I chose a few different seats, my back remained facing the wall.

Another factor in my discomfort was the relative lack of the usual medical role. Without the protection of a traditional mode of operating I had an acute sense of exposure and vulnerability. Also, by doing something outside of my usual doctoral duties, it was clear from 'joking' comments that some people around the hospital were thinking I might be a trifle odd! I think some of the patients known to me felt something similar, but a few with whom I was in regular contact became acutely interested in me. They were clearly wondering if, after all, I was so very different from themselves.

At the time one of the ways in which I overcame this discomfort was to create a new role for myself. I became a detached observer, undertaking some kind of academic exercise. I saw myself as a champion of the patients' complaints about their conditions in the canteen (which were frequent) and, for the nurses, someone who might be able to ease their difficulties in the canteen – this being one purpose of my investigation, as I thought. It was only some time after completion that I was able simply to value it for the experience of being with staff and patients in a way totally different from anything that I had been trained in or taught before. It had also given me a different insight into the life and work of the hospital.

THE OBSERVER

Much of my contact with staff and patients was hesitant and restrained. Nurses with whom I had a prior acquaintance would check that I had received some message or other.

One senior nurse, with whom I had a good relationship, said 'Here you are doing your observation – punishment, more like!' He sat with me talking of his duties – the care and protection of some of his more elderly patients. We chatted quite freely, but that did not seem appropriate and I maintained some coolness behind my observing duties. He was giving me information about his duties here, and from his initial comments I realised how he felt about it – under some strain.

After many weeks, one young nurse came to me very apologetically asking what I was doing and saying that some nurses were asking who I was and 'was

I all right?' I managed some reply about 'observing' and 'a project', at which he quickly thanked me and withdrew, both of us none the wiser for the experience.

My position there seemed to be immediately understandable if I had some special role.

As for the patients, a young girl with a severe psychotic illness often sat with me, at times booking her seat by placing some article on it beforehand. She was often very thought-disordered and it was extremely difficult to hold or follow a conversation with her. She seemed to misidentify me with someone from her past and I largely kept my distance.

During one of her bizarre monologues, however, she very aptly said, 'You look very fine in your steel castle.' This described exactly my attitude to her and I was too surprised to take the point further.

On another occasion, she commented on a young man who, shouting abuse, threw his tray onto the floor saying 'Oh, he's just fed up waiting in the queue. I feel like that sometimes.' This comment also came in the midst of irrational and disordered speech.

She was clearly able to make empathic contact, but for the most part seemed to be miles away. My view of her as someone with a severe psychotic illness seemed to close off any thought of her other qualities, hence my surprise when she made remarks which did not fit a stereotyped view of her condition.

THE NURSING STAFF

In keeping with the general atmosphere in the canteen, my main perception of the nurses was as a police force, and some form of challenge and confrontation was not infrequent. This produced some difficulty for me; should I become involved if some disturbance happened near me? It did not feel comfortable to be an observer and become involved in policing, and so I left this to the nurses. But no serious disturbance actually happened, despite the atmosphere of almost constant expectation of trouble. However, when there were incidents, it was clear that many, both patients and staff, had difficulty in exercising a control function. There was no sense of collective responsibility – the power to control a situation was seen as residing in only a few of the nurses (the more senior psychiatric nurses), the others seeming rather helpless.

On one occasion, a young man had taken an item belonging to a female patient who was very distressed. She complained to him, then to the nurses

who were also unable to persuade him to return her property. They sent for a
male nurse, who quickly made the man return the item. He then patrolled
around the canteen for a short time looking carefully about him and left. The
nurses who had called him were very appreciative in their comments.

Obviously, they and the male patient saw only this nurse as able to enforce
the request.

Care, treatment and control are all elements in the management of
patients, but it is still difficult for some to accept responsibility for control in
particular (Bott 1976). The majority of the nurses in the canteen were
general-trained nurses which, although common in the rest of the hospital,
was a cause of critical comment by some senior nurses – they complained
that some of their colleagues were avoiding these disturbances. Within the
canteen itself there was some relief when someone clearly visible was
available to take over this function. The nurses as a whole were clearly
uncomfortable and congregated in two groups near the doors, also with their
backs to the wall. Conversation was very largely restricted to that between
the nurses and was often about external, unrelated matters. Contacts with
the patients as well as myself were much more hesitant and unsure.

The 'crash of plates' illustrates this well; it was a regular occurrence,
always producing a momentary hush. My expectation at these times was
that some form of conflict was about to ensue which made one freeze. I
understood from the similar reaction of others that this was a fairly general
expectation – despite it repeatedly being disproved.

On one occasion, an old lady dropped her tray out of sight of the large group
of nurses. When no further disturbance occurred, the nurses continued their
conversation. However, they were prompted into investigation when a nearby
patient sarcastically remarked 'I see the nurses rushing to help.'

Another time, a patient, well known throughout the hospital for violence,
seemed to collapse shouting in the queue. She was engulfed by nurses who
escorted her out, leaving relatively few behind.

These two apparently different incidents in their context seemed to lead
to a distancing of the nurses. The first involved an obvious withdrawal
(until it was painfully pointed out); the second, perhaps a sanctioned way
out of the canteen – leaving with the disturbance.

The nurses' discomfort could be transmitted to others. The young girl
who often sat by me afforded another example one day, to the annoyance
of a fellow patient:

As that fellow patient eyed me suspiciously, she announced that she needed
some salt and obtained it from a table next to his (perhaps to rub it in). This
led to an angry exchange between them, during which she punched the air. A

female nurse detached herself from the group and led her back to her seat urging her to 'eat up'. The girl began talking of sexual matters in a very disjointed way, which increased the nurse's urgings. The nurse was now directly behind me but moved to stand by the patient's side, between us, and the girl lost interest in the food and stood up. The nurse placing her hands on the girl's shoulders then gently but firmly guided her out of the canteen. The nurse – whom I did not know, or she me – obviously felt that the girl was at some risk and was anxious about this. I became equally uncomfortable when she stood behind me, but was unable to make any comment that might have eased the situation.

One could see attempts at making more comfortable contacts, but they usually failed, being only fleeting eye contacts and smiles. A nurse sat with a few patients who were from her ward and made three separate attempts at conversation. These all received minimal acknowledgement and she left looking bewildered and dispirited.

CANTEEN STAFF

I had no direct contact with the canteen staff and it was difficult to form any impressions about them. There certainly appeared to be a fair number of them and they all appeared very busy behind the serving area (their steel castle?). They rarely came out to the dining area to collect the plates until the end. The nurses identified them as terrified of the whole experience. Their contacts with patients were often coloured with bad temper and some indifference. Perhaps the most striking feature was that serving was always ten minutes late. It is not clear why this was so, but it certainly added to the tension already present and contributed to the development of the queue. At times the staff would protest and refuse to serve the patients who pushed to the front of the queue. These patients, however, were usually young and rather intimidating; they would fairly soon be served, as if to move them on, confrontation being perhaps too difficult to sustain. Of all the groups present, the canteen staff seemed the most distant, having an area that was exclusive to them and rarely venturing from it.

THE PATIENTS

The patients formed the largest group of people in the canteen. The majority were always silent and seemed to be 'just passing through'. The silence of the patients was striking, most of the conversation coming from the two groups of nurses. There was, however, a smaller group of patients who were boisterous and noisy, also conspicuous by their relative youth.

They flouted many of the 'rules' in the canteen, pushing into the queue and smoking. Protests from other patients were usually muted and ineffective, and only some nurses were able to gain their co-operation. Although these noisier patients often congregated together, much of their activity was solitary. Many roamed around the dining area looking from patient to patient. Their gaze was usually avoided, and when I came under scrutiny, it certainly felt uncomfortable:

A large, imposing West Indian stood above me for some time but when I eventually looked at him and nodded a greeting, he smiled and moved on to repeat the exercise elsewhere.

The fear of violence seemed to stem especially from this group, and they were often in conflict with the nurses. It was not, however, that they were overtly violent, but that their intrusiveness was felt as a violent attack. This was my experience with the patient just mentioned; I felt distinctly abused until our mutual greeting removed this. On watching him repeat this with a number of others, the quality of the interaction seemed to be the same.

In thinking of the larger group of patients, one is reminded of the term 'silent majority' – carrying on life, hopefully free from outside interference. It was not uncommon to see people unashamedly pull up their knickers in full view, or belch loudly on sitting with other people, neither of which actions seemed to gain any response. One chap sat opposite me and produced from his pocket a filthy handkerchief, which contained his dentures. He was quite oblivious of my aghast stare and no one else gave him a second glance.

Distance from the nurses could be clearly seen in the way that tables near their group by the entrance were used much less than the others.

It was possible, however, to see small groups of patients and couples who regularly appeared, giving, although not obviously communicating, some support to each other.

Two old ladies seemed inseparable. On one occasion, they wandered through an upturned dinner on the floor, slipping and sliding, until they sat at a table at the epicentre of the mess. No one else was using it at the time. After about fifteen minutes, a nurse cleaned up the floor, apart from that beneath the old ladies who remained unmoved whilst he cleaned around them.

To initiate conversation in such an atmosphere was difficult and attempts were infrequent. Some patients, however, approached people with a proposition, such as, '10p for a fag', but moved on after the exchange.

On one occasion, a patient wrote out a Christmas card and gave it to each of the two ladies just mentioned. They politely thanked her, glanced at each other and continued eating. The patient who had written the card remained quiet and soon left.

As previously noted, one of the most striking features of the place was the enormous queue that formed, often persisting to quite late on in the session. This was a constant source of complaint around the hospital and it was suggested that wards should have staggered eating times. This, however, never seemed to filter through to the canteen, the queue remaining as long and as silent as ever. A fair number of patients were escorted in by nurses; they were sat at a table and the nurses obtained their food for them by themselves going to the front of the queue. The initial impression of these patients was that they were too unwell to have to queue; indeed, most appeared rather frail. It became apparent, however, that many were able to eat unaided and would leave by themselves after. Were they too frail or just 'playing the system' and avoiding what seemed to be one of the most uncomfortable aspects of the canteen?

One patient who clearly needed assistance was confined to a wheelchair, deaf and blind. During one observation, he proceeded to shout a string of jokes, laughing heartily after each one, perhaps as if to provide his own audience. The only feedback he received consisted of clearly embarrassed pats on the back from his attendant nurse. She seemed quite uncomfortable at the attention being directed towards them. However, apart from a few short-lived glances and smiles no one seemed very bothered.

It was rather ironic that someone as inaccessible as this patient should be providing such a public display.

CONCLUSIONS

One of the striking features of the canteen was the similarity in the atmosphere of each session. This persisted despite the frequent comments of staff and patients as to the great discomfort they experienced in being there.

Menzies ([1959] 1988), in a study of the functioning of a nursing service, has described how its social organisation serves as a defence against anxiety. This function may be primary in the development of such organisations, the ultimate purpose of the service representing only a limiting factor to its structure. She identified particularly defensive techniques which rely on evasion as being paramount, but noted their lack of success in dealing effectively with anxiety, and their tendency to produce more, secondary to the operation of the defensive system. Menzies' study as well as other contributions to the dynamics of health care institutions are described in more detail in Chapter 1.

The rigid atmosphere of the canteen was maintained by a number of defensive techniques. These centred on the obscuring of people's individuality and the resistance to change in the system.

Emotional withdrawal puts considerable distance between people; they tend to be identifiable only by group membership, as patients, staff, etc. No single person is left to face the anxiety alone. This seemed to be reflected in the close proximity the members of the respective groups appeared to keep. This was very divisive in that it was possible for a group to project disavowed aspects of their own experience into another. The nurses, for instance, saw terror and fear well and truly located in the canteen staff. Although this appeared an accurate observation, these emotions were not alien to themselves. It seemed to be easier to have others bear these feelings, but it seriously inhibited the nurses from being able to confront and master these feelings adequately.

There was considerable routinisation of activity: the queue, the late start, and people's general behaviour and reactions. Little seemed to influence this; Christmas came and went unacknowledged by decorations, so familiar elsewhere in the hospital. The routine also proved resistant to change. A rota system was devised to stagger the times at which patients from the various wards ate. However, no one carried out these new guidelines and the large queue remained unchanged.

In considering the underlying nature of the anxiety I would like to return to the fear of contagion by mental illness. Patients of all kinds frequently project their anxieties and worries onto hospital staff. Indeed, this is an important aspect of the functioning of the hospital. However, how this distress is processed and contained is vital for the effective functioning of the service. Conran (1985) describes this phenomenon, making the point that if the patient is unable to hold onto these parts of himself at that time an interpretation of events might best be made to the attendants, to aid their management of the situation.

It is not an uncommon idea that mental illness has an intrusive, damaging effect on those in close contact with it. This certainly describes the quality of contacts made in the canteen. My experience with the young West Indian typifies this. However, it was possible to change the nature of that interchange to something far from the fearful and damaging expectation described above.

The degree of anxiety was markedly higher in the canteen than in other areas of the hospital. This is, I think, related to the extent to which the defensive system was threatened there. In turn this is possibly related to the number of unknown patients and staff whose roles could not easily be categorised and who therefore felt more naked and defenceless as individuals.

The notion of the conformity of mental illness is very common. Indeed, there are relatively few diagnostic choices and treatments, and very often they appear interchangeable. It is, however, worth noting that the blurring of individuality may be more related to the defensive attitudes adopted by those with, and those working with, mental illness.

These observations on defensive techniques may also be extended to the acrimonious debate concerning community care which was taking place at the time this observation was carried out. If one considers the structure of a mental health service in terms of anxieties and defences, it is not surprising that a change in the system of delivery will evoke much anxiety because long-established defensive techniques are stripped back. There has been little attention to basic fears and attitudes about mental illness in the debate about structural changes. These, however, need to be considered if change is to be anything more than symptomatic. A new style of service, based on the same foundations as before, will suffer the same limitations. Or to put it differently, if within a new structure there is no greater possibility of containing the anxieties of working with mentally ill people, then the resulting system will be equally defensive. The observations in this book that were carried out in mental health settings after major changes had been implemented (Chapters 5, 6 and 7), indeed confirm such concerns.

Finally, to return to the canteen: one change did occur after the study was completed. This was the introduction of plastic knives and forks and paper plates – a further symptomatic change, dominated by the defensive system of evasion. The new eating implements have impoverished an already Spartan atmosphere, while the difficulties experienced by those who attend have remained unnoticed and unattended to.

Chapter 5

At a crossroad between institutional and community psychiatry

An acute psychiatric admission ward

Marco Chiesa

INTRODUCTION: THE CHANGE TO COMMUNITY CARE

Over the last two decades the thrust towards shifting the focus of care provision for the mentally ill from the hospital to the community has gathered pace (Harrington 1988; Coid 1994; Dobson 1998). The mental health resource centres located in the community, with their emphasis on multidisciplinary work and with a declared focus on the integration of biological and psychosocial aspects of mental illness, seem to have substituted for acute admission wards as the places which are felt to provide a sense of achievement and fulfilment to staff. In addition, a scarcity of acute beds to fulfil local needs has meant a substantial increase in pressure and workload on staff located in hospital settings. There has, therefore, been a growing sense that staff who work in the community are more privileged than those who have been 'left behind' in wards.

The perceived differences between the two settings may cover a more complex reality (VV.AA. 1998). Leaving aside the actual merits or failures of care in the community, it is a fact that a high percentage of patients who used to be treated in the admission ward are now cared for within the community. Consequently, ward staff now look after the most disturbed amongst the psychiatric population. This brings greater demands and stress, which is not matched by an increase in therapeutic success. Many psychiatrists, social workers and occupational therapists spend an increasing amount of time in community centres; they are therefore less available to nurses, who may feel less supported in looking after such highly disturbed patients, so that feelings of demoralisation set in. The relative devaluation of hospital ward work was probably more noticeable in acute wards within psychiatric hospitals, because they are more affected by the culture of the large institution. The district general hospital or teaching hospital psychiatric units may still maintain a sense of worth and fulfilment due to their links with – and greater possibilities within – the general hospital.

In this chapter I describe the results of an observational study carried out over ten years ago, consisting of weekly 90-minute visits to an acute admission ward within a large psychiatric hospital in London.

Although there are many comprehensive studies of organisations (Stanton and Schwartz 1954; Miller and Rice 1967; Miller and Gwynne 1972; Bott 1976; Selvini-Palazzoli *et al*. 1987), live ward observations have the advantage of an observing professional not directly involved in the running of the ward, which allows fresh understanding of events and interactions between patients and staff (see Chapter 2; also Hinshelwood 1989 and the observations collected in this book).

Psychiatric institutions were originally built with the intention of providing a safe physical environment for the mentally ill, who were removed from society, cared for, treated and – ideally – discharged back to the community. However, the process never turned out to be so simple and straightforward, as demonstrated by the growing number of patients who became long-term inmates of such institutions. The phenomenon of chronicity tended to be conceptualised as belonging solely to the patient's illness: a function of a progressive organic pathology within the brain or untreatable intra-psychic resistance towards change. The pioneering ideas of Pinel (1801), Conolly (1856) and Bleuler (1924), suggested the influence of the social structure of the institution on the patients' behaviour, symptomatology and prognosis. And this was eventually more systematically investigated (Barton 1959).

METHOD AND AIMS OF THE PROJECT

The method of observational studies within institutions is described in detail in Chapter 2 of this book. As discussed there, the observations and the inferences made on them are necessarily subjective. The observer enters the complex social entity of a ward once a week for a short time, with no knowledge of the ongoing internal situation, and this considerably limits his inferences to hypotheses about his institution's phenomena. I will expand on this issue later in the discussion.

Three main aspects seemed to emerge from my observations on the ward:

1   The way in which serious anxieties, feelings of guilt and sense of responsibility were dealt with by patients and staff, through the use of psychological defence mechanisms such as projection, splitting and denial, operated through subtle interactions, channelled and reinforced by the institutional structure within which these interactions took place.
2   The existence of a collusive culture within the ward which fostered stagnation and lack of movement, and militated against constructive activity.

3   The prevailing atmosphere on the ward, the quality of interactions
    among patients and between patients and staff, the way in which the
    ward structures were used by patients, the feelings evoked in the
    observer: all seemed to confirm a change in the quality of the work
    within the hospital acute admission ward. In turn this shift may result
    from the different quality of the patient population admitted, due to
    the effect of community care policy in the previous decade.

Other authors (Hinshelwood 1987a; Menzies [1959] 1988) have previously illustrated the first two points. The observation of a change in the
quality of the population in admission wards is first documented here and, I
think, represents the major contribution of this chapter. This finding also
demonstrates the contribution which observations of this kind may make to
documenting phenomena that might otherwise go unrecognised or remain
at the level of subjective speculation.

The study of the dynamics of an admission ward offers a possibility of
comparison with other studies carried out in chronic wards. A cross-study
comparison would confirm, add or disprove assumptions about differences
in atmosphere between acute wards and chronic wards.

In this study I did not adhere rigidly to any preconceived model, which
could become too restrictive and lead to a degree of selective blindness in
the researcher. I approached this project with an open mind, first recording
what I observed without superimposing my biases, and only when the study
was finished did I set out to analyse the data. My broad theoretical framework relied on the concept of social defence system (Jaques 1955; Menzies
[1959] 1988), as described in more detail in Chapter 1 of this book, and on
that of 'open system' (Miller and Rice 1967).

SETTING UP THE PROJECT

As discussed in Chapter 2, the preliminary stages in setting up a project are
important because they determine the way in which the members of the
organisation accept the researcher and, in addition, yield preliminary
information about the state of the organisation.

I first approached the heads of the medical and nursing disciplines in
writing, briefly explaining the nature of my research and asking for their co-
operation in the matter. Only one of the two consultants replied to my
letter, after a considerable delay. I met the other consultant after I con-
tacted him over the telephone; he conveyed a polite interest in the research,
wishing to know more about what it would entail. The nursing officer did
not reply, and I had to pursue him. He was very kind; he had no objection
to the project, and added that he was going to have a word with the ward
sister, whom he suggested I should meet.

When I went to the ward to meet the ward sister, she was very friendly and welcoming, and expressed considerable interest in my proposal. She showed me round the ward, introducing me to the other nurses. In showing me two empty rooms, she complained in a resigned way about the slowness of the administration in equipping them adequately for the purpose of patients' rehabilitation – that is, acquiring decent social skills through task-oriented work. She explained to me how difficult it was to motivate patients to do anything, and that this difficulty was exacerbated by the lack of co-operation or interest from 'others' in the hospital. As the visit ended, the sister volunteered to let other staff know about my future involvement with the ward. In addition, I wrote to all members of the medical team to inform them about the nature of my weekly visits to the ward.

From this initial contact, a passive attitude was shown by the professionals in charge who did not respond to communication, even though they showed enthusiasm once I managed to get hold of them. With hindsight, it is possible that nursing staff felt trapped between, on the one hand, patients who were unmovable and unrewarding to work with and, on the other, an unresponsive hierarchy which turned a deaf ear to their requests for help. As Menzies ([1959] 1988) illustrates, the nursing staff's perceived predicament might be the result of a mixture of reality and phantasy. The latter stems from an upward projection of guilt and responsibility, starting from the patients and leading up to the administrators via the nurses and doctors, while feelings of irresponsibility are projected downwards through the same channels.

FEELINGS EVOKED IN THE OBSERVER

One of the anxieties I initially felt about the project was related to my own position in the ward, in the passive role of an observer. I would have to sit for 90 minutes in the lounge of an acute admission ward, observing events, behaviour and interactions (or the lack of them), which would inevitably involve me emotionally. I doubted that I would be able to contain and process feelings and emotions evoked in me in the course of the observations, while having no opportunity to engage in either verbal or non-verbal communication.

Doubtless, the most difficult feelings were the ones evoked by the stilted and impersonal atmosphere which permeated the ward most of the time, as I will shortly describe. The flattening of human contacts, the stifling of creative activities and the predominance of apathy evoked in me feelings of depression and hopelessness that were difficult to tolerate. After a while of sitting on my chair I would feel restless inside, wanting to move and do something active, or get up and leave out of exasperation. At other times I realised that I was coping by absenting myself mentally, caught up in phantasies and thoughts that had no connection with the task in hand. On occasions I experienced feelings of despair about the usefulness and meaningfulness of my project, and became very angry about the possibility that I was wasting time. In this scenario of gloom and isolation, I welcomed the odd interaction with a patient. However, I also experienced sorrow, sadness and sympathy for the patients and felt a wish to try to help some of them out of the miseries their mental illness was putting them through.

WARD OBSERVATIONS

When I arrived for my first visit I was asked by the acting charge nurse to identify myself. He seemed surprised by my presence – evidence that at least some of the staff had not been informed about the nature of my visits. As it turned out, the patients had not been informed either. After clarifying my position, the acting charge nurse told me that a patient who had been sent on short leave from the ward a few days earlier had committed suicide, and that this event would be brought up during the community meeting which had just started. The reaction to the announcement that a patient (Paul) had been found dead at his home was one of chilled astonishment. Some patients asked brief questions about his physical appearance in order to identify him; a cold silence followed. Then a nurse expressed worries about George, a patient present at the meeting, who had a large sutured cut on his head, following deliberate self-harm. After a very uncomfortable silence, the student nurse who was chairing the meeting said that she would be leaving the ward the next day for a Mental Health Resource Centre in the Community, as part of her rotational training. Silence followed. A patient's statement that the telephone box was out of order was met with a quick assurance by a nurse that everything possible was being done to repair it. At this point, prompted by a patient's comment, the group's attention returned to Paul and this time more people contributed with questions or comments. Some patients expressed concern about Paul's girlfriend, herself a psychiatric patient, who had been sharing a flat with him. The two patients who had joined the meeting late and were sitting outside the group joined in to make a full circle. The rest of the meeting was characterised by the rather noisy and bizarre talk of a floridly psychotic patient (Martha), which remained unaddressed, while other patients thanked the student nurse and wished her good luck in her new placement. Before closing the meeting the nurse announced that George was not to leave the ward unescorted, and she sought other patients' co-operation. Some patients tried to bring up other issues at the eleventh hour in an attempt to stop the meeting from ending.

Soon after, the TV was switched on rather loudly for the rest of the morning. A few plastic glasses fell from the tray that Martha was carrying; in a fit of temper she threw the whole tray on the floor and left, swearing, through the main entrance. The nurses quickly intervened to pick up and clean what had been spilt. Martha, who appeared to be very irritable and restless, then brought the tea trolley into the lounge. Patients very quickly gathered around the trolley and helped themselves to tea, using large amounts of milk and sugar. George asked for a razor in order to shave; he was given an electric one for fear that he might harm himself. Patients were uncommunicative with each other, either restlessly going in and out of the lounge, or sitting motionless on their chairs gazing into space or at the TV set. Throughout this part of the observation, no nurses were present in the patients' lounge; they seemed very busy in the nursing station or in other parts of the ward. A patient remarked that nurses were not available to respond to a request coming from George. The fragmented and feelingless atmosphere changed slightly towards the end of my observation when the TV broadcast a programme on the River Ganges. A clear, warm voice described in touching and poetic prose, with soothing music in the background, the religious and symbolic meaning of the Ganges for the Indian people. Many patients changed their expressions from an apathetic and absent one to one of interest and hope.

In this observed sequence of events it seemed that staff and patients reacted and interacted with one another under the pressure of an anxiety-provoking situation which deeply involved both, albeit at different levels. The staff members' anxiety led them to be overactive in carrying out their duties, perhaps to convince themselves and each other that everybody was doing their utmost. In this case, however, such efficiency seemed to be divorced from contact with the patients, and the ultimate effect was their distancing from the patients' group. Even though the student nurse who chaired the meeting was a containing and competent person who did not panic in the face of such a dramatic event as suicide, it was interesting that she was left to handle this difficult situation, while more senior nurses were engaged in other activities. The suicide must have evoked internal phantasy situations of one's depressed and suicidal parts, which were felt to be located in George. This blocked the possibility of mourning, and staff's anxiety was directed towards activities aimed at preventing a fresh incident. Would staff have been so solicitous with George if the suicide had not occurred? They reacted to possible feelings of guilt and responsibility for the suicide of a patient by becoming over-strict and over-conscientious.

The patients' attitude was characterised by a mixture of withdrawal and inertia, and by mechanical responses to the experience of the death of a fellow patient whom many of them had met. They complained of the faulty telephone box, which might indicate unconscious awareness of the communication difficulties they were experiencing, leading to most of them withdrawing in a helpless, cold and robotic silence.

Eventually, after the group was able to return to the dramatic news, they could do some processing of the event through the gradual identification of the dead man. It is probable that through her style of leadership the student nurse conveyed to the patients a sense of solidity, straightness and warmth, which allowed some containment of the anxieties evoked by the suicide. They clung to one another in the group in the face of disaster, and found it difficult to relinquish their clinging identification, as shown by their reluctance to stop the meeting. As the meeting ended, they regressed to isolation, apparently oblivious of environmental stimuli. A testing of the staff's capacity to contain feelings of pressure took place when Martha dropped the tray. This event represented the enactment both of the patients' inability to hold onto the emotional burden triggered by their fellow patient's death and of their wish to relinquish a sense of responsibility by spilling over their feelings onto staff members. On this occasion staff responded promptly, without taking any custodial measure. The moving moment when patients' attention was drawn to the programme about the River Ganges was of some comfort, because it gave an indication of the presence of a responsiveness to something life-giving and meaningful.

Heartening moments like the one described above were rare during my observations, and generally a rather deadly, cold and impersonal atmosphere permeated the lounge. There was a heavy sense of sameness and timelessness, in which the flattening of human contact was a constant characteristic, week after week. The impersonal sounds of the TV, the electric razor, the vacuum cleaner, the stereo and banging of doors dominated the scene. The TV in particular was constantly switched on, broadcasting soap operas or light entertainment. Many patients were staring at the box, but it was difficult to understand whether they were actually following the programmes. Time and time again I found myself being drawn into the TV set like metal to a magnet, while my mind was wandering elsewhere.

The fear of becoming like one of those patients, on the surface devoid of any emotion, may have been present in staff, at least at a preconscious level. On more than one occasion I saw the timid and uncertain attempts of student nurses trying to make contact with psychotic patients being rebuffed or not responded to. After a while the nurses would give up, take on themselves for a moment the patient's immobile, dejected and apathetic posture, and then proceed to leave the lounge, not to reappear for quite some time. The avoidance of contact with the patients, which may have resulted partly from the chronic frustration of the nurses' attempts and partly from fear of recognising one's own psychotic or depressed parts, was a constant observation during my stay on the ward. However, this avoidance was selective for patients suffering from chronic schizophrenic disorders, while nurses concentrated their efforts on less damaged patients, who were more responsive to their approaches. Contacts between patients were rather brief and temporary, often consisting of requests for – or offers of – concrete objects, such as cigarettes or food.

Once a female patient (Maria) sat next to a male patient (Jack) and tried to talk to him in a warm way. Having received a smile in response, she took his hand in hers and smiled back at him. Two people holding each other's hand evoked a reaction in the other patients sitting nearby, who started to talk to them in a way that interfered with their closeness, and soon the two were separated.

The hatred of anything warm and creative found its expression in the stifling by one or other of the patients of originally spontaneous initiatives (table-tennis match, card-playing, and so on), or in the passive rejection of proposals for common activities (taking a walk or going to occupational therapy). The operation of deep-seated envy may be one of the roots to the patients' unresponsiveness to the nurses' efforts to provide help, and to the obliteration of any affect and activity. The patient group did not tolerate someone else's enjoyment, which they themselves did not have, and proceeded to spoil it at the outset. The attacks on the nursing staff's capacity to offer help seemed successful and the defeated nurses retreated, believing that they were unworthy and not good enough. The maintenance of a flat atmosphere on the ward, where little of interest could happen, was, at the same time, a defence against envy: in a desert there is hardly anything worth envying.

This atmosphere of deadness, lethargy and apathy was in sharp contrast with the sense of industriousness and overt expression of emotions that seemed to predominate at times during the 90 minutes of my observation. I soon realised, however, that this was the other side of the coin: the expression of a manic state that seemed to infect patients and staff alike. People were restless, coming into and going out of the lounge as if they were busy carrying out tasks, or as if their actions were goal-directed. Interactions were quick, fleeting, superficial and hypomanic in mood similar to the touch-and-go behaviour described by Donati (1989). The mood was shallow and unpleasantly facetious – staff joined in with remarks, which fed into the elation; the TV was loud, the stereo blasted rock music, and a few patients danced clumsily. The sterility of those aimless activities seemed to be a reaction to the inertia and passivity described above.

WARD MEETINGS

At the outset of the project I chose a time and a day for my weekly observations not knowing the schedule of the ward meetings, in which most patients and some of the on-duty nursing staff participated. Once a staff nurse mentioned to me the meeting in the course of a short conversation, and I took the opportunity to ask him how often meetings were held. He replied that they usually lasted half an hour and were held weekly – but not usually on the same day, for it was dependent on enough staff being present on the ward. This meant that patients never knew when a meeting would be called until the last moment. As it happened, ward meetings were held during 11 out of 16 visits I made. They never started at the same time and their duration was ranging from 20 to 35 minutes. The staff present generally included two or three student nurses and one staff nurse; the ward sister and the psychiatrists did not take part. It was often unclear who chaired the meeting, for at times a patient called an agenda, but soon a staff nurse would take charge, encouraging people to participate and bringing up issues for discussion. In these meetings a characteristic repetitive pattern became evident. The pace of the meeting was slow, mainly due to the patients' passivity, which evoked anxiety and restlessness in staff. They felt pressurised to step in, and took over in an attempt to generate something constructive. As staff became increasingly active, patients' passivity and inertia grew proportionally which in turn increased anxiety in the staff who, as a result, tried desperately to force activity onto the meeting. Their failure to produce any response led to reactions of frustration, anger and desperation in nursing staff. Typically, after a community meeting in which nothing constructive was achieved, no meeting would be called the week after. Staff who saw their efforts constantly turned down seemed to have given up, at least temporarily, the hope that a creative culture could be generated. Yet staff attitudes contributed, in an unconscious collusive fashion, to the maintenance of a status quo in which constructive activity and movement were reduced to a minimum, as borne out by the following example:

During one community meeting a student nurse questioned whether the TV should be kept switched on all day long, as she noticed that it prevented people from interacting with one another. She proposed that it should either be switched on for only a limited number of hours during the day, or moved into the subsidiary lounge. Many patients supported this view, only one or two voices timidly disagreed. At the end a final vote was called, and the outcome was that the majority were in favour of the TV being moved away from the main lounge.

The student nurse had succeeded in challenging the tyranny of the TV set, and most patients had responded positively. What was left undecided, however, was when, and who should take the responsibility for moving the TV set. After the meeting was over it was dutifully switched on as if nothing had been decided. The decision was never carried out, and the issue was never brought up for discussion again. In a similar vein another positive decision reached by the members of the ward meeting was ignored: that a patient rota to keep the ward kitchen clean should be drawn up.

In these examples staff, for some reason, did not use their authority to make sure that decisions were implemented; they therefore actively participated in fostering a culture of stagnation.

The most common form of intervention by patients in ward meetings was to complain about aspects of life in the ward – for example, that the toilets were dirty, that there was not enough soap or toilet rolls, that the food was not good or too hot or not enough, that the telephone box was in the wrong place, and so on. This is an illustration of the dependent assumption (Bion 1961) of the patients' group, who passively brought up complaints with the expectation that staff would resolve them. The collusive aspect of this culture was that the nurses felt that they did have the responsibility to meet patients' complaints, and consequently felt under pressure to put everything right immediately. Facing this unrealistic task created defensive reactions in the nursing staff, who tended to deflect the blame on to other professionals (domestics or administrators), or to turn their backs on the patients.

RESPONSES TO MY PRESENCE

When I started the project I was wondering how staff and patients would react to the presence of a person who entered the ward weekly, sat on a chair for 90 minutes, and then left. As initially agreed with the ward sister, I had assumed that staff had been told who I was, and about the general purpose of my visits.

The second time I visited the ward and sat in the lounge I found a completely different set of nurses. After a while the staff nurse who was acting for the absent sister came towards me and asked me to identify myself and clarify my reason for being there. Later a patient (Gerry) asked me who I was; to my reply that I was a doctor he commented that I might have been sent to the ward to keep an eye on patients.

There seemed to be a discrepancy between the way I was being perceived by staff and by patients. The former inquired rather suspiciously about me, seeing me as an intruder. Patients saw me as a protective, super-egoish figure, a perception that might have arisen in connection with the patient's suicide a week earlier. This incident also showed that not all the staff had been informed about my weekly presence on the ward, revealing some lack of communication among nurses.

I feel that my presence stimulated staff to try harder and to show their resilience in interacting with very damaged people. One staff nurse came to me after a difficult ward meeting, and remarked in a rather apologetic tone that meetings were usually more constructive than the one that had just ended. The sister was always very welcoming and solicitous towards me (I described her openness in our preliminary meeting above). She kept reminding me of the feedback to the ward staff I had agreed to give after the project was terminated. I think that she idealised me as someone who might have great understanding of the nurses' ongoing difficulties, and might at the end provide them with a solution. The experience of an external psychiatrist observing their work did not on the whole seem to evoke excessive suspicion or persecutory withdrawal, and some staff showed a positive attitude to my interest in the ward. At the end of a particular observation two staff nurses expressed disappointment when it was explained to them that I was meant to spend only 90 minutes there and not, as they had imagined, the whole day.

Most patients seemed to ignore my presence, even though they often gave me quick glances, which conveyed puzzlement, suspicion and fear. Some of them would test me out by creating a disturbance in my vicinity, or by coming towards me in a menacing way and insulting me, only to leave me alone when they realised that I would neither react nor be scared. In each observation I had, on average, two or three direct interactions with patients. I will describe one of these, because I believe it is instructive about aspects of psychotic functioning:

A patient who had shown a considerable degree of schizophrenic thought disorder decided to sit next to me and asked me who I was; to my reply she said that she did not believe I was a doctor; she thought that in reality I was a policeman in disguise. She proceeded to talk to me in a disjointed and seemingly unconnected way about her family, her life and her present circumstances. Then she decided to make me a cup of tea, which I accepted. She drank hers in one go, while I put mine on the table after a couple of sips, as it was too sweet for my taste. When she asked me if I did not want it any more, I offered my cup to her, assuming that she wanted it. She became very irate with me, shouting that I did not want the tea because I suspected that she might have poisoned it. Later she came back and brought me a rose.

We could look at her paranoid reaction from different angles, but I want to focus on one aspect of what happened between us. The patient perceived correctly that I did not like her tea and sensed that I had not been honest with her. My action of offering her my cup seemed unselfish (I was seemingly depriving myself to give her my tea), but in fact it had a very different underlying motive: I offered the tea because I did not like it. Then this correct perception was turned into the delusion that I thought she had put poison into my tea. Embedded into her delusion, however, was the communication that she had correctly perceived my deceptive way of relating to her.

DISCUSSION

Until recently acute admission wards were regarded as places where rewarding psychiatric work is carried out. Patients' turnover was relatively rapid, the majority of patients being discharged back home after a short period of hospitalisation. The staff–patient ratio was much higher than in chronic wards, and psychiatrists, social workers and psychologists, who also had duties in chronic wards, spent most of their time in the admission ward (Bott 1976).

The mushrooming of mental health centres and other facilities in the community has offered an alternative to hospitalisation for acutely disturbed patients, who are preferentially treated within the new resources. Now the patient who is admitted to an acute psychiatric ward is likely to present with more entrenched and long-standing psychopathology, although not of the same degree of chronicity characteristic of long-stay patients. Therefore, the move towards community care seems to have selected a discrete sub-group of patients who are neither chronically ill nor deemed fully treatable in community mental health centres. This shift in the quality of the population in admission wards has had a negative impact on the morale of ward staff, who are now dealing with – on average – more intractable patients than they were ten or 20 years ago. Staff see fewer positive results from their efforts to help these patients, which leads to an increasing sense of futility and worthlessness. The current relation between the admission ward and the community mental health resource centre is mirroring the relation that had existed between the chronic ward and the admission ward. The recent emphasis on community care has created a shift and a new balance that may be expressed by the following equation: the chronic ward was to the admission ward what the admission ward now is to the community centre.

If my findings are compared with those found in observations in long-stay wards (Donati 1989), some differences between the two settings do emerge. First, the physical environment of the admission ward is cleaner and more modern, with more facilities; this makes it more pleasant to live in. On the surface, there is more interactive behaviour among patients and between patients and staff. The logistics and policies of the admission ward favour comings and goings of patients, staff and visitors, giving the onlooker less sense of stagnation than is the case with chronic wards. However, strong pulls towards the flattening of meaningful human interactions, the pre-empting of potential constructive activities, the predominance of apathy over enthusiasm and a wish to defeat attempts to create a positive culture were constant features of my observations. The consequent lifeless atmosphere, which often permeated the ward, bore strong similarities to Donati's descriptions. Even the sense of busyness observed on the ward at times seemed for the most part to represent a manic reaction in order to bypass anxieties about fragmentation, worthlessness and hopelessness. Sinanoglou (1987) observed the attitudes of staff in a psychiatric unit; she found that they needed to be involved in perpetual commotion and activity to combat basic fears of becoming lifeless, empty and lethargic.

What I have described seems to support the view that acute admission wards have taken on similar features to chronic wards, and that similarity between the two settings has been far greater since the advent of community care. Other similar studies are needed to confirm that this trend may not just be episodic, or confined to the ward I studied.

Another factor that greatly influenced the quality of the atmosphere in the ward was the implementation of a policy of nurse rotation in the whole hospital. As a way of tackling the high rate of sickness absenteeism, it was decided that every day some nurses from fully staffed wards should move to badly affected wards to give temporary cover. This created great uncertainty in staff nurses, who would not know where they would be working each day – that is, whether or not they would be moved to a different ward. These incessant and unpredictable moves greatly disturbed the nurses' continuity of care for their patients; this unsettled both patients and nurses, decreased the nurses' job satisfaction and increased their anxiety. The patients felt disoriented and confused by these continuous changes, which flawed even further their already limited capacity to form a relationship with nursing staff. The disturbing effect of this policy predictably increased sickness absenteeism, creating a vicious circle. To borrow a quotation from the Palo Alto group: 'the attempted solution has become the problem' (Watzlawick and Weakland 1977).

I would now like to turn my attention to the role of the observer and the method used in this type of study. As I explained above, the observer sits in the ward, for a fixed period of time, as unobtrusive as possible and limiting to a minimum his own interactions with the surrounding environment. His aim is to record events, moods and interactions as they become manifest before his eyes. All this is done to attempt to reach a state of neutrality in the observer. I think that the word 'neutral' may be misleading because it implies that the observer's presence does not have an influence on the environment being studied. Rees (1987) states that the observations he reports are not objective, for the observer is subject to the atmosphere of the setting. Bick (1964) explains that the method of infant observation was developed as an adjunct to the teaching of psychoanalysis and child therapy, rather than as a research instrument. The idea of an objective reality which is not affected by the presence of the observer has been challenged by the sociology of knowledge (Berger and Luckmann 1971), by radical constructivism (von Glaserfeld 1984) and by the new cybernetics (von Foerster 1982). These schools state that we cannot conceive of an external reality without taking into consideration the observer's function in creating it. Reality is not conceived as independent of the observer's efforts (physical or psychological) to organise it. For example, Freud's original concept of transference, which is activated not only onto the figure of the therapist but also onto the other aspects of the patient's life (Freud 1914), adds strength to the notion that what is observed also results from the observer's presence and activity. Transference and countertransference phenomena are intimately bound together, and the verbal and non-verbal behaviour of therapist and patient would become an artificial object of study if we tried to separate them (Chiesa 1989). Indeed, I believe that my presence in the ward did affect patients, staff and myself as the observer.

These considerations, however, should not imply that inferences made from observational studies are not valid. Rather, it is important to realise that what is under study is a system which includes both observed and observer. In particular, a great deal of attention ought to be paid to the multi-level influence that the observer has on the observed, and to the way in which what he is observing will affect the quality of his observations. In other words, two aspects have to be taken into account: first, the observer's possible distortion of his observations; second, the observer's subjective involvement as the essential component of the observation. Only a fine line separates the former from the latter; it is therefore important for the observer to be supervised and to have the opportunity of discussing his experience in order to be able to disentangle what results from which of the two aspects.

The observer focuses on a limited field – in this research a part of a ward – and has no access to other important areas which might render what he is observing more explicable. For instance, I could make sense of some of my observations by my knowledge of the policy of nursing rotation and awareness of the recent thrust towards community care. It might be possible to improve the research methodology, following two different directions. The first would be to set up a longitudinal study in which four or five different acute admission wards were observed by the same researcher. The results could then be compared with data from chronic wards and from community resource centres. The second would also include individual interviews with medical and paramedical staff, administrators, patients and their relatives. The information thus obtained can complement the hypotheses generated by a non-active observer.

Chapter 6

Mental and physical space
A long-stay psychiatric ward

Judith Edwards

INTRODUCTION

In this chapter I describe the process and content of an observation study undertaken in the lounge of a long-stay psychiatric ward on the day of the patients' weekly ward round. I chose this method to investigate the patients in this setting as I believed it might give me a more personal understanding and awareness than that which could be derived from more structured systematised methods.

There were many reasons why I found myself drawn to and interested in this group of patients, most of them were related to the impact that community care might be having upon them. I had previously worked in this hospital when the number of in-patients had been much greater. I knew that despite the moves to empty the asylums, there still remained a residual number of long-stay patients who were considered too disabled for community care, and who were thought to be in need of long-term rehabilitation.

I found myself thinking about these patients and what it must be like to be a resident on a long-stay ward. What was the emotional culture like, and what was the quality of the patients' social interactions? In another setting and in another role, I had been involved in the care of long-stay patients who had been successfully discharged into the community. They had all appeared to settle well into their new environment, but had often remarked in the first few months how much they missed their previous hospitals or asylums. I thought then that the quality of life in such asylums might have been socially richer and more satisfying than would first appear. A ward observation study offered me a 'way in,' to test out my hypothesis.

After finishing the study, however, I was surprised to find that I could only think about the observations in a fragmented way. It was difficult to know where to begin, how to try to put the pieces of the jigsaw together, and how to try to evaluate and understand the experience. I found myself wondering whether I had introjected aspects of these patients and had come to identify with them, hence my paucity of thought; yet it was extremely difficult to develop these ideas further.

THE CONCEPTS OF 'POTENTIAL' AND 'ILLUSORY SPACE'

I was eventually helped in this, my psychological journey, by concepts developed by Winnicott and Milner: Winnicott's concept of 'potential space' and Milner's one of 'illusory space'. These then became my theoretical anchoring points, but were ones which I could only use after the observations were complete.

Milner referred to what she called the 'illusory space' in her book *On Not Being Able To Paint* (Milner 1950). The 'illusory space' lay at the interface of inner and outer reality, between what was internally conceived and what was externally perceived. She suggested that it was here that creativity arose from the difference between the inner and outer worlds. This space, if subject to early developmental trauma, could fail to develop, leading to a restricted creativity and inner freedom.

Winnicott's thinking was influenced by Milner's, and in his paper 'The Location of Cultural Experience' (Winnicott 1967) he described what he called the 'potential space'. This too was located at the interface of inner and outer reality, the inner psychic world and the outer world of objective reality, the environment.

Winnicott suggested that the capacity to engage in this area varied between individuals, and was dependent upon a good enough relationship with a maternal object at an early stage in development. It was in this potential space that play was located, which could then expand into creativity and culture. If subjected to severe trauma, this space could fail to develop, and could instead be massively impinged upon by the outside world. This could lead to a diminished space with impoverished thinking and creativity.

In this chapter, I explore two separate but related themes. In the first I use my observations to look at the patients' use of external physical space – the ward environment. I suggest that this relates to and expresses the patients' use of internal mental space, which I then relate to the illusory, potential space, which I suggest has been diminished. The theme of place emerges as an alternative way of describing the physical space, which I suggest is particularly pertinent to this patient group. I then go on to discuss what I understand to be some of the differences between space and place – in particular, that of place being a part of the space.

The second theme relates to my own illusory or potential space. I suggest that in the process of observing, this space had also been diminished. At the completion of the observations my data felt overwhelming, fragmented and difficult to think about. I had gathered many impressions, thoughts and ideas but found that they lacked coherence and cohesion. I wanted a defined format and structure to help order the chaos.

Further ideas of Milner, outlined in her *On Not Being Able To Paint*, were very helpful and provided another anchoring point, the central theme of which is that the purpose and direction of her writing and painting only became evident during the actual activity of writing and painting. It was only when she allowed herself to paint spontaneously that she became truly creative.

Similarly, I decided that I needed to write spontaneously about the observations and thoughts which naturally came to mind, and that this process might enable me to understand my experience more fully. Indeed, the actual process of writing, which I found difficult, seems to have been an attempt to struggle against the emotional impact of an experience (which had diminished my potential space), in order to rebuild a creative space within me, where I could have thoughts and ideas. An alternative title for this chapter could have been, 'On Not Being Able To Write', and the eventual writing of it could be thought of as a sort of 'working through'.

THE SETTING UP OF THE OBSERVATIONS

Having chosen the type of patients I wished to observe (the long-stay schizophrenics: the 'graduates' of the asylums), I then needed to locate a particular ward and gain permission for the study.

I first introduced myself in writing to the medical and nursing directors of the Rehabilitation Directorate, requesting a meeting with each in order to discuss my proposal and gain permission for the observation. I followed up these letters with several telephone calls, and was eventually advised by the medical director to meet the nursing director.

There then followed a long and useful discussion with this senior nurse who outlined the structure of the Directorate and its wards. I had not known that there were five wards, each catering for different needs within a long-term population of chronically psychotic patients. All of the patients were being rehabilitated, and the time-scale for this varied. One ward was locked and particularly catered for those with 'challenging behaviours', whilst another ward specifically cared for older patients with additional physical disabilities. I had previously been unaware of these differences.

The nursing director suggested that I observe Ward X, an open ward where the rehabilitation was termed 'slow stream'. These were very-long-stay patients, but ones for whom there was still an expectation that they could eventually be discharged into the community. She noted that these patients usually had both 'positive and negative' symptoms of psychosis (delusions and hallucinations but also apathy and amotivation), but that it was generally the negative symptoms which limited progress. The nursing director was interested in the study and enjoyed telling me about her wards, but nonetheless seemed bemused, as if wondering why I would want to observe her patients.

We agreed that it was essential that I have some preliminary meetings with the ward staff, prior to commencing the observations. I was able to visit the ward twice. On the first visit I was proudly shown around the ward by the ward manager. The ward had recently been refurbished and it was pointed out that all patients now had their own bedrooms with doors which locked. I arranged to be present the following week at a nursing handover, when both morning and afternoon shifts would be present, in order to introduce myself and explain the purpose of the study as well as to agree the days and time of the observations.

Despite the staff's stated interest, there appeared to be some uncertainty and anxiety about my role; two staff nurses wanted to know exactly who I would be observing, as if they feared that I would be there to observe them. I sensed anxieties which could not be expressed, and which my words would not be able to allay. At this stage the ward manager stepped in, in a firm authoritative manner, and gave her nursing perspective and approval to the study. This appeared to reassure the staff nurses, who might also have been worried by my being a doctor. This could have related to the nature of the doctor–nurse relationship, possible professional rivalries and differences. As if to further support my work, the ward manager then suggested that such observations could be usefully fed back to the staff once the study was complete.

SETTING AND METHOD

This was a rehabilitation ward for men and women in a psychiatric hospital built in the late nineteenth century. The patients had all been diagnosed as chronic schizophrenic. All had been hospitalised for more than five years, and some for more than twenty. The ward was an amalgamation of two wards, which had been developed along a shared corridor. It had been refurbished when given its dual status one year earlier. This dual ward had one nursing office, but two lounge and dining areas (A and B), both of which were open to access by all the patients.

My observations took place in lounge B, which was part of a much larger room. It was demarcated from the dining and kitchen areas by four rows of chairs arranged along three walls and across the room to form an inward looking rectangle. A television set occupied one corner of the room and a radio another. There were small tables in the opposite corners, home to several ashtrays and an odd assortment of newspapers.

I sat in lounge B for an hour a week for 12 consecutive weeks on Wednesday mornings from 9.30 a.m. until 10.30 a.m. Wednesday was chosen because it was the day of the consultant psychiatrist's ward round, when patients were expected to be present on the ward in case they needed to be seen. During this time the ward staff were usually preparing for the ward round. The patients' coffee break was at 10.00 a.m., and the ward round commenced at 10.30 a.m., the time at which I would be leaving.

My aim was to sit on the ward and observe the patients in their normal setting, trying to register both objective observations and subjective feelings. My field notes were recorded after each observation and discussed in a supervision seminar. The observation method itself is described in more detail in Chapter 2 of this volume.

FINDING MY PLACE

I vividly remember how anxious I felt on that first day, and my thoughts at the time. These mainly related to a fear that my unannounced entry into the patients' lounge, their home, might be interpreted as a hostile act. I was also very self-conscious and uncertain about how I should enter the lounge, where I would sit and how I should behave.

On a preliminary visit to the ward, when the arrangements about the observations were being finalised, I had decided that I would sit in lounge A in preference to lounge B. Lounge A was more spacious than lounge B and offered easier access to the corridor and a more direct exit from the ward. At that time this felt safer. However, when I started the observations, I found lounge A empty of people, which lounge B was not. I then made an immediate decision, which surprised me, to sit in lounge B instead. Lounge B, a smaller more restricted space, now felt safer and more secure than lounge A and was a space into which I defensively retreated.

The original quandary about which lounge to sit in was then followed by which chair to sit in. Once again I made an immediate decision and chose to sit well within the patient group alongside the wall opposite the entrance and the corridor. This position enabled me to see easily all those who entered and left the room, but also was fully inside the patients' external space, the ward environment. In many ways it was as if I felt the need to both physically and emotionally decrease the distance between me and the patients, as if too great a distance would engender severe anxieties which could relate to our differences. Perhaps I unconsciously needed to minimise our differences by blending in.

On that first morning I found only two patients in the lounge. They were sitting next to each other along the wall nearest the door and corridor. Betty, who appeared to be in her mid-sixties, was dozing. She wore costume jewellery, red nail varnish and make-up. Her neighbour, Janet, was considerably younger, in her forties, and appeared less institutionalised. She wore a wedding ring and a light anorak with the sleeves pulled up. They gave me indifferent glances. Meanwhile, two older male patients negotiated the exchange of cigarettes in the dining area. They too seemed indifferent to my presence.

After about thirty minutes a male nurse entered and asked me if I ran a group. I replied: 'No.' That was the first spoken interaction I had had and seemed to be the cue for a male patient, 'Paul', who had entered the room with the nurse, to speak. He commented on my shoes and legs and seemed disturbed by my presence. He eventually decided to introduce himself and to shake my hand. He then left to have a bath, having been prompted by the male nurse.

Meanwhile, Betty and Janet continued to be silent and appeared unconcerned about me. Eventually, Betty, after about fifty minutes, spoke to Janet: 'What is she here for?', and she replied: 'She just sits.'

During that first observation I was intrigued by how little I seemed to have impacted on the ward and its residents. Betty and Janet had 'just sat', as I had done, each in the same place. I had been worried about how they would perceive me, and yet they had shown very little curiosity about me and my intentions. Their restricted use of the external space, the ward environment, by doing nothing but sitting and hardly even looking, could be understood as an expression of their limited internal potential space in which they could be playful and explore.

Paul had seemed to be mainly interested in my shoes and legs, but apart from a handshake, had communicated by speaking at rather than to me. Although he had introduced himself, it did not feel as if he wanted, or was able, to create and maintain a dialogue. It felt as if Paul had found our emotional contact difficult, albeit exciting, and one which he needed to move away from, 'to have a bath'. This was in contrast to Betty and Janet who stayed in the room, seemingly unaffected by my presence. They remained in the same chairs and places, which I suggest both expressed and allowed them a limited emotional stability.

BEING IN DIFFERENT PLACES

From the beginning, the act of finding my place in lounge B had been important. As the weeks progressed it became increasingly so. For ten of my 12 observations I felt fortunate that I was able to sit in the same chair (place) and chose to do so. Even when the room was crowded that chair remained vacant, and it felt as though the patients had reserved it for me. I felt relieved and reassured by this, and found myself wanting and needing 'my' place to both physically and psychically anchor me. Indeed, on the two observations when I had to sit elsewhere, I felt awkward and anxious.

I believe that the need for their own place was also important for these patients. I never knew how many patients in lounge B were from this ward, as their number varied between none and 20. Some seemed to be visitors from other wards, who might drop in for a cigarette and a drink, particularly at coffee time when the drinks trolley was wheeled out. However, there was a group of five regular 'seniors' who were consistently present in the lounge during my observations and who obviously resided on the ward. They were the older patients, in their sixties, who appeared to be more chronically debilitated than the rest. There were four males and one female within this group.

Each senior generally sat in the same chair and place each week, although occasionally they would sit elsewhere. The following two vignettes illustrate how different places within the lounge appear to have different social and individual meanings for the patients.

In the first, a patient negotiates the return of his chair from another patient, and changes places.

George, a patient in his mid-forties, entered the lounge. He appeared cheerful and eager for emotional contact. He approached John, a well established senior who was in his usual seat. John appeared to be asleep, although a half-smoked, unlit cigarette hung from the corner of his mouth.

As George approached, John opened his eyes. George lit John's cigarette and was rewarded with a beaming smile, after which John again closed his eyes. George then sat down alongside John and said: 'Your seat, mine?', the first words to be spoken in their encounter. Thereafter, for about five minutes, they changed seats again and again, as if this was a game of musical chairs. Both appeared enlivened by this encounter, although John had initially been reluctant to move. Finally, John settled in his original chair and then refused to move. George, who was still restless, left the lounge.

I was struck by how emotionally alive George and John appeared during this playful encounter. Their enthusiastic activity seemed temporarily to light up the room. However, this in itself had created an anxiety, particularly for John who then needed to retreat to his own inner world and the concrete security of his own chair, which seemed to anchor him both physically and emotionally. It was as if any meaningful emotional contact with another was felt as precarious and dangerous. John's potential space had not been able to sustain the emotional contact with George.

In the second vignette, Betty chooses different chairs and places within the lounge according to her emotional state.

Betty, as a senior, usually sat in one particular place. However, in the fifth observation I found her sitting in the dining area although 'her' chair was vacant. She was obviously troubled and uncharacteristically intervened in an upset between two younger patients over cigarettes. She tried to protect Frances from Sam who had demanded Frances' last cigarette. Betty shouted at Sam and then physically attacked him, much to the other patients' amusement. Sam then left the room. Betty then went to her usual chair, but after five

minutes suddenly stood up and came towards me, angrily shouting and wring-
ing her hands. She sat down three chairs away from me.

This action seemed to trouble her even more, because she then moved to sit
next to me. I was concerned both for and about her, and although I did not
speak, wondered why she wanted to sit next to me, and what would happen
next. Our concern appeared to be mutual. She asked me if I was all right, and
then put her arm around me. I replied that I was fine. She seemed to feel more
settled and contained by this, and moved back to her usual chair. For the rest
of the observation she appeared settled and returned to her normal slumped
posture, in which she appeared to doze.

In this observation, Betty occupied two or more places, both psychically
and physically. In her usual place and chair, she was relatively at ease,
compared with the rather persecutory state seen elsewhere. Much as she
needed the physicality of different chairs in order to express her emotional
state, it seemed that she needed bodily contact to emphasise and convey her
emotional communication.

My understanding of her response to me was that she had projected parts
of her damaged self into me, and was trying to care for me as she felt the
need to be cared for. Her attack on Sam could also be understood as
reflecting her own perception of being under attack. I found myself feeling
very moved by her caring and attempts at reparation, which had a childlike
immediacy about them.

In subsequent observations she was always in her usual place. She made
no further comments to me, or about me, apart from telling some visiting
patients: 'She is new, but has been here before.'

INSIDE AND OUTSIDE

Throughout the observations I had found the patients indifferent to my
presence. They enquired little about me and appeared to experience me
almost as one of them. For many, their use of external space appeared to be
restricted and focused on a life inside the ward and hospital. However, in
the ninth observation, Janet, who had previously noted that 'she just sits',
did fleetingly enquire about me and 'out there'.

Janet greeted me as I entered the lounge with a cheerful 'Good morning.' The
day was pleasant and sunny, late spring. She said: 'Is it warm out there?' I
replied that it was. She then asked if I was a doctor on the ward, and I replied in
my usual semi-truthful manner: 'No, I am here as a visitor.' She then asked:
'Do you live outside?' I said yes. She smiled and then appeared more reflective.

Soon afterwards, Janet asked Bert, a fellow patient who had been wander-
ing in and out of the lounge without ever sitting down, for a cigarette. Bert

nodded and Janet joined him in the centre of the room. This was a signal for Bob, a senior, to join them. The three patients then huddled together like children in a playground. Bert silently gave a cigarette to Janet, and another to Bob, each of which he lit with his own cigarette. Bob in turn gave Bert a cigarette paper. Bert and Bob said nothing, but Janet quietly said 'thanks'. Afterwards they separated and wandered off to smoke their cigarettes alone.

I detected a wistfulness and sadness in Janet, and was struck by her quiet dignity. What must it feel like to live inside an institution and to be, day in day out, with carers from the outside? What did the concepts inside and outside mean? She had once lived outside but had had to come inside; yet she was on a rehabilitation ward with the aim of going outside again. She seemed accepting of her non-outside states, but for a moment appeared to be in touch with her own tragedy and sadness, particularly at the point when she had allowed herself to become aware that I was not a patient and was different from her. The anxiety that this interchange engendered seems to have been the cue for Janet to ask another patient for a cigarette. After speaking to me, she needed to link up with other patients like herself. The familiar inside world of patients and cigarettes presumably felt safer and less threatening than our interchange, which made her painfully aware of the outside world. I, in turn, then felt that I was in the presence of an all exclusive club, which had its own rituals and ways of relating, and that I was on the outside. This being on and from the outside had a different quality to that when I first entered the lounge. Then, in a spirit of enquiry, Janet had asked about and recognised our differences; but later, it felt as if I was being avoided and rejected because of the associated emotional pain, as the patients literally turned their backs on me. My feelings of exclusion at that point probably mirrored Janet's as being excluded from a life outside.

THE CULTURE OF THE PLACE

My original quest had been to become more aware of this, and as the study progressed certain aspects registered more than others.

The overwhelming impression was of an interactive impoverishment in which verbal communication was severely restricted. Often it felt as if the content of the words mattered less than the emotions associated with them. When John and George played musical chairs, all that was said was 'Your seat, mine?' Much could be conveyed by very little.

However, the patients had other ways of communicating. Cigarettes were especially important, and presented opportunities for verbal and physical exchanges and rituals. They were the principal currency of communication and were used in a variety of ways: to console, soothe and control. The last vignette – 'Inside and Outside' – illustrates this.

The television and radio were usually both switched on at the same time. Generally no one appeared to pay any attention to either, but occasionally a particularly restless patient would frantically change channels, although this occasioned little or no response from those around. I had several thoughts about this. I wondered whether this 'white noise', which I found irritating, was soothing for the patients and acted as a distraction from difficult inner and outer worlds. Perhaps the sounds helped to quieten their voices. A further thought was that the patients identified with these fragmented sounds, which represented aspects of themselves, and that this was their way of communicating verbally via another medium. This being talked at, rather than talked to, would be less threatening than a dialogue with another person. Changing the channels, or even switching off the TV or radio, could be understood as an attempt to control both the outer and the inner world.

Within this culture of a restricted social intercourse, the place, via one's concrete position in the room, became very important as I have described earlier.

CHANGES IN THE WARD ENVIRONMENT

While the patients generally appeared indifferent to me, as I just sat as they did, their reaction to other changes was more marked as the following examples show.

In the seventh week, at the start of the observation, three window cleaners arrived on the ward. They were young male representatives from the outside world and were obviously very different from the ward's usual residents. Before their entrance, the lounge was virtually empty, with only two patients present. Before starting work they were brought to the lounge by two female nurses and shown the windows. This seemed to act as a magnet, and within minutes the lounge was filled with spectators, male and female.

Then, in what I felt was a defensive manner, the cleaners worked in a fast and furious way, as if displaying their superior masculinity and potency. They did not talk to each other nor the patients. Eventually, after five minutes of frenetic activity and poorly cleaned windows, they left hastily and jauntily, almost strutting. Their departure coincided with an eruption of restlessness, irritability and agitation, most evident amongst the male patients.

The window cleaners initially appeared nonchalant and detached from the obvious excitement they had engendered within the patient group. This excitement felt rather brittle and superficial, with undercurrents of hostility. It seemed as if both they and the patients were overwhelmed by anxieties.

For the cleaners, it may have been about their unease at working in the midst of mentally ill people who were watching them intently. The cleaners may have had fears that mental illness might contaminate and infect them. For the patients, the window cleaners' presence was a rather intrusive reminder of how different they were from these visitors.

Some of this disturbance may have related to the rather sexualised quality of the cleaners' 'act'. They had been introduced and shown the windows by young female staff, and had then performed and worked out before an older and emotionally damaged audience, none of whom could work or just leave.

Further examples show how relatively minor changes in routine could also upset the patients.

In the fifth week, a new domestic lady arrived, whose method of distributing the morning drinks differed from her predecessor's. Previously, the drinks trolley was wheeled out into the lounge where drinks were dispensed. However, this domestic insisted that those who wanted drinks had to come and collect them from outside the kitchen area. This caused a lot of grumbling amongst the patients, which the domestic ignored. To me, the observer, it seemed as if the patients resented not only the change but also the need for them to be more active in getting their drinks.

I also noticed how restless the ward was following a Bank Holiday weekend, when several regular nursing staff were away. This reinforced upon me the need for consistency and constancy in caring for and working with these patients. Changes in routine, however trivial, could be, and were, perceived as threatening.

These reactions to minor changes could be understood as confirmation of how restricted these patients' potential spaces were, and how necessary a familiarity and sameness in their external environment was for them.

LEAVING MY PLACE

This was much more difficult than I had anticipated. I had become emotionally attached to the ward and its residents, in particular to lounge B which felt like a temporary home. I was sad about a leaving which had no rites of passage. I was surprised by this as I appeared to have made little impact on the ward. I had aroused some curiosity, but had been asked relatively little about who I was and what my purpose might be. Unlike the window cleaners, I had simply been allowed to be there.

Perhaps the patients' apparent indifference towards me related as much to my need to 'blend in' as to their need to minimise the anxiety that a recognition and an awareness of our difference could engender. My just sitting, as they did, and having no perceived easily recognisable role or function, no doubt facilitated this.

Maybe my sadness at leaving reflected their own sadness about leavings and past losses which could scarcely be articulated or acknowledged. Certainly, these patients' observed sensitivity to change would suggest that at a deep level they were more aware than they appeared, and that their indifference was a defensive organisation.

As the study progressed, I found that I, like some of the patients, had become attached to 'my' chair and place within the ward. In observations 10 and 11, I had to sit elsewhere and was ill at ease as I was literally 'out of my place'. It felt fortunate that 'my' chair was unoccupied for the final observation. This constancy of place helped me to enter and leave the lounge that day.

AFTERTHOUGHTS AND DISCUSSION

Many thoughts came to mind once the observations were complete. I was struck by how difficult it was to think about and organise the experience and the data, and how paradoxical it felt to be both overwhelmed and emptied by it. I was unsure about how I would structure and understand the experience. It had felt valuable and in many ways a privilege simply to be allowed to be with these patients in their ward home. I thought that I had become more aware as a result, but what exactly did that mean? One understanding could be that my state of mind was linked to that of the patients, and that my confusion and paucity of thought reflected theirs.

Eventually I decided (in the spirit of Marion Milner) to just get on and write about those observations which naturally came to mind, and to see where this would take me. The ideas which then emerged, by conscious and unconscious distillation, related to the themes of *place* and *space*. At times it was difficult to distinguish between the two concepts and articulate a difference.

Place became the predominating theme and emerged more easily than that of space. Place can be understood as both a verb and a noun, a process and a location, with individual and group meanings. The two *Oxford Dictionary* definitions of 'place' which seem particularly pertinent are: 'part of space occupied by a person or a thing' and 'proper natural position'.

I found that 'place' was important because it related to my need to find a physical place and proper position within the ward environment, but also for that of the patients within the ward hierarchy.

It would appear that Betty and John were in different mental states in different places, and this had both individual and group meanings. The observations also showed that the seniors usually occupied the same chairs, and that the more restless patients tended to position themselves furthest from the centre of the lounge. Particularly agitated patients seldom sat down (the image of an atom came to mind, with electrons revolving around a nucleus in varying degrees of stability).

In comparison, the concept of *space* took longer to develop and emerge but was facilitated by the process of writing. 'Space' is less easily quantifiable and discreet than 'place' and perhaps this is why Winnicott and Milner used the term to describe the intermediary area; Winnicott, of course, emphasising its potential quality and Milner its illusory nature. The three *Oxford Dictionary* definitions of 'space' which seem relevant to this study are: 'a limitless area that surrounds all objects', 'room', and 'something measurable in length, width or depth'.

Certainly space and place are linked, as the latter can quite literally be part of the former. As previously noted, I was very aware of the patients' limited use of external space, the ward environment, and their observed need and mine to have a 'place' within the ward.

I suggest that 'place', then, has both meaning and intention. The meaning is that it is an outward sign and expression of a limited internal space and thereby potential space. However, the act of attaching and clinging to the 'place' is also a primitive attempt to both physically and psychically anchor oneself in order to try and rebuild a potential space within.

Winnicott suggested that the foundation of this potential space lay in early development and the infant's relationship with the mother. In pathological states, there is a massive impingement from the external world which forces on the mind the presence of a 'not me' world and destroys the illusion of omnipotence. As a result, the potential space collapses, and the 'continuity of being' which Winnicott regarded as the foundation of the ego is ruptured. Once this continuity of being is broken, and the ego fails, then the individual's problem is how to capture a sense of self. He does this by either withdrawing into the psychotic world or by clutching at the external world. There is also a marked incapacity for creative play and symbolisation.

Aspects of this were seen when George and John briefly changed chairs again and again. This seemed to be a rudimentary attempt at creative play which John, the older, more deteriorated patient could not sustain. This play was mediated via a concrete change in place, with virtually no verbal communication. As with Betty, it was as if John used different places and chairs to express different states of mind. It is notable that when John broke off the emotional interaction with George (at a point when he felt himself to be massively impinged upon), he could only do so by returning to his own chair. John had clearly been disturbed and overwhelmed by the emotional exchange which his restricted potential space could not support. I suggest that this then led to a loss of a sense of self, which led him to retreat internally, but also to cling externally to his particular chair and place. This had both meaning and intention.

Marion Milner suggests that awareness of reality is a creative process involving a complex interplay between inner and outer reality in the illusory space. This involves an interchange of difference, and is associated with mental pain, which will vary according to the individuals' emotional development. In the early stage of emotional development this will involve magical creativity and annihilation, and in the later, conscious and unconscious love and hate for the object, with the need to protect and make reparation.

These ideas enrich how we might understand the patients' limited creative capacities. They might also reflect their restricted potential space, which cannot sustain and tolerate difference and ambivalence, curiosity and reflection. The impingement of the 'not me' world then collapses the potential space and the continuity of being. This results in a defensive withdrawal into their inner worlds, where they can magically and omnipotently rule, and a primitive clinging to a physical concrete place.

CONCLUSION

The main findings to emerge from my observations related to the themes of place and space, with their consequent effect on the individual and the group. As an individual, I had observed a group (of individuals) and in so doing had discovered that the environment of the ward had affected me. My sense of place and space had become muddled, and I initially had great difficulty in thinking about the experience. I suggest that this related to a partial collapse and restriction in my own potential space, and an associated loss of self. I relate this to the observation process, and the way in which I suggest I was being pressed into having a similar experience to that of the patients.

This led to a need, both in myself and the patients, to find and know our places within the space of the ward environment. The concrete external place can then be understood as having both meaning and intention. The meaning becomes an expression of a psychic place, which by definition is limited and restricted: its intention is an act which helps to restore a creative potential space within. Indeed, knowing my place helped to create the structure for which I had been searching. The process of writing also helped.

The knowledge which I gained was neither objective nor subjective, but had developed in my potential space, and had been achieved through my own activity and experience. I found it a valuable way of 'knowing' these patients, and believe it gave insights which other approaches could not. Certainly I gained considerable satisfaction and relief in struggling through the difficult work of digesting an experience which had restricted my potential space, but eventually emerging with an expanded capacity to think and 'play'.

Chapter 7

Tyrannical equality

A mental health hostel

Mark Morris

This chapter describes an observation project carried out in a community based mental health hostel. The methodology and psychodynamic basis of this observational approach have been described in detail in the introductory chapters of this volume. I shall first try to describe why I wanted to see what happened in this sort of setting, then present some process material, from the setting up of the project and selected material from the actual observations. Finally, in the discussion, I will present a hypothesis and draw some tentative conclusions.

WHY A MENTAL HEALTH HOSTEL?

The professional reason for wanting to observe a mental health hostel in the community was because of changes taking place in the provision of care of the mentally ill at the time. When this project was being carried out, and over the time that I was in psychiatric training, British psychiatry was in a major state of change from the provision of care in the in-patient setting of large hospitals to a community care model. This approach was meant to provide a network of facilities, including day hospitals, mental health centres or 'clubs' and community hostels, with hospital beds being increasingly reserved for patients in the acute stages of their illnesses. As a trainee, one was regaled with accounts of the poor culture and environment in the large asylums (Chapter 3 gives an example of such a culture). The plight of chronic patients sitting like statues in front of daytime TV with nothing to demonstrate the passage of time except drug rounds and changes of nursing shift, is indeed difficult to bear. It seemed to me that awareness of these problems spurred on the reformist zeal to community care, which would change patients' lives for the better. Critics of this sort of asylum care cited the inhumanity of the back ward 'human warehouses'; critics of community care argued that asylums, albeit institutionalised, were better for patients than their slipping through an inadequate community care net and ending up on the streets.

Somewhere between these two extremes lay the mental health hostel which seemed to be better from two perspectives. Funded by the local authority, the mental health hostel, unlike the large asylum, actually was part of the community. And, staffed and run by social workers and associated care staff, the culture of the organisation would be clearly social rather than medical. Residents would be people with difficult backgrounds or in crisis rather than 'manic-depressives' or 'schizophrenics'. This would combat the slip into inhumanity that can occur when a patient becomes a diagnosis rather than a person. Also, the strict medical hierarchy and associated paternalism of hospital care accelerating the descent into institutionalism would be replaced by a more normalising social care model, where resident and staff groups are both members of the wider community. Thus mental health hostels provided places in the community for patients whose residual deficits were too severe for them to be contained in the community. The hope was therefore that patients living in a hostel would benefit from being part of the community, and yet have basic needs supported, with pro-fessional staff available to fall back on if required.

The personal reasons for wishing to observe a mental health hostel were more complicated. As a psychiatric trainee with an interest in the psycho-dynamic perspective, I found myself very aware of and open to the suffering of patients with mental illnesses. Endless erudite debates about whether patient X was schizophrenic or manic depressive seemed irrelevant in the face of the agonising and terrifying experiences that they faced. The con-ception of 'negative symptoms of schizophrenia' seemed to trivialise the tragedy of an ill-kempt man in an ill-fitting suit shuffling around the hospital grounds; the tragedy of the life that could have been. The reduc-tion of insane people's complex, shifting and terrifying experience into a medical diagnosis seemed over-simplistic. An alternative seemed to be the social models of mental illness, and I had the opportunity to work for a year in the Barnet Psychiatric Crisis Team. Set up in the 1960s when the anti-psychiatry social critique was influential, the Barnet Crisis Team model was that the identified 'patient' was a symptom of a dysfunctional family or system (Scott and Starr 1981). Intervention was at this level instead of a more traditional medical model where treatment is directed at the patient. Even so, in spite of the evangelical application of this more humane and dynamic approach, people still became psychotic, and insanity was still unbearable.

I began to see the 'isms' in mental health care as displacements from the simple fact that mental illness is unbearable; that working with people who are losing their minds is unbearable. The sense of deterioration and unbearability that plagued psychiatric hospital back wards did not reflect the abuse of the mentally ill from this perspective. The unbearability of the psychiatric hospital back ward reflected the awfulness and deterioration that is mental illness. From this perspective, the function of the new mental health philosophies and models of practice was not to improve the lot of the mentally ill, but rather to manage the despair of the workers and provide the illusion of progress in an area where progress is slow. Scull's (1977) 'decarceration' of the mentally ill from the asylums seemed to me to have this quality of occupational therapy for the carers and ignored the legitimacy of asylum as a refuge for those in distress and unable to focus on self care.

As my psychiatric training progressed, I gradually became persuaded of the legitimacy of a medical model of insanity. To me, it provided an ideological structure in which the overwhelming experience of working with the mentally ill could be contained. I began to wonder whether the clear and unambiguous perspective of the medical model of insanity might also be containing for the mentally ill. For the psychotic who believes that they are responsible for the Holocaust, being labelled as schizophrenic reframes their experience so that it is more containable. They are not responsible for the death of six million, but instead they may have to take anti-psychotic medication for a few years. As well as this, the social structure of the hospital hierarchy – doctors, nurses and patients, all with their roles and expectations – was constraining and paternalistic, but it provided boundaries and a framework for people whose internal psychic structure had collapsed. If the medicalisation of mental illness provides a social and ideological structure which contains the chaos of mental illness, the social perspective of dismantling these structures seems like a rather precarious venture. If the hospital social hierarchy contains some chaotic aspect of insanity, what will happen if this is removed?

So for personal and professional reasons, an interest in observing a community hostel grew. Most of the settings that had previously been explored using the observational methodology had been in and around the hospital, but with the decanting into the community many of these were now gone. The proposal to carry out a project in a community based hostel not only addressed my own questions about medical and social models of psychiatry, but also seemed to be a logical next place to look in the broader sweep of projects that had been carried out thus far.

FIRST IMPRESSIONS: DISINTEREST AND INTIMIDATION

Hospital social service contacts provided the names of two community hostels, both of which I wrote to. My letter briefly described the psycho-dynamic observational methodology and explicitly stated what the project would mean in practice; namely, the observer visiting weekly for three months and sitting unobtrusively for an hour. After a delay and no response, I followed the letters up with telephone calls, one of which was returned. In the telephone conversation with the manager he seemed interested and psychodynamically informed. After a further delay and chasing up by telephone, he suggested I visit to discuss things further. A date was arranged when I would visit.

The hostel was set in a small 1960s low rise estate of local authority housing which had an air of neglect. The hostel building itself was relatively new and apparently purpose built, but the door looked as though it had been broken and fixed several times. The impression of siege or battles fought was amplified by the fact that it was securely locked and that I had to wait some time before the buzzer was answered.

It was eventually opened by (apparently) a resident who unlatched it without saying anything and left me in the hall unattended. The place seemed deserted. (I learned later that at ten in the morning, everyone was still in bed.) After some time I introduced myself to a busy looking man who walked past, explaining why I was there, and correcting his assumption that I was a psychiatrist arrived for a consultation with one of the residents. With some thought, he remembered that he had heard about my request. Steve, the manager had been off sick for some weeks now, but he was acting manager, and would be able to see me in a few minutes. After a further wait, I was led into a staff room where we spoke for about half an hour and then I was shown around.

The resident group of 30 was managed by a staff group of about fifteen on a shift system; mostly 'care workers' supervised by social work staff. Referrals were taken from a variety of sources, and the model was that they stayed for a period of 12–18 months of rehabilitative work before being moved out to less dependent accommodation. In practice, some residents stayed longer, and the work of the day seemed to be more preoccupied with dealing with crises. The day before there had been a problem with a drunken and violent resident, necessitating a visit to the local casualty department. The staff member complained that once a resident had been accepted, it seemed that psychiatric backup was withdrawn, and the hostel was left to get on with it. I found myself feeling responsible and wishing I could prevail on senior psychiatric colleagues to respond and admit the hostel's residents sooner.

Being shown about, the environment seemed a curious mixture of modernity with open cast brick walls, and dilapidation, with heavily used furniture, a broken front door and ubiquitous untidiness. The building was arranged around a central television/dining room with a hatch to a large kitchen and an area with a pool table. Two sets of corridors led off twenty-five or so bed-sit rooms on two floors with staff rooms on the ground floor. Staff were friendly, introducing themselves, but the residents who were around seemed blank. In the discussion it emerged that I was to present my proposal to the resident group, who would make a decision about whether I would be allowed to carry out my project. I was told that it had been discussed in the social services management hierarchy, and provisionally agreed. In this initial meeting, there was also a preliminary discussion about suitable visit times and where I might sit to observe. There was also a sense that I might be able to contribute something back to the staff group about my findings, as if the staff group were framing the project as an organisational consultation. I agreed that, if they wished, I could meet them to feed back some thoughts on completion, although interestingly this never happened.

As agreed, I wrote to the residents' chairman, and was invited to attend the residents' weekly evening business meeting to present my proposal.

On the night, after again waiting some time to get in, I was ushered to an office by a man who said he would get Steve, the manager. Several moments later, a young man with a scarred face and skinhead haircut, wearing a shell suit, came in and started using the phone. Unable to get through to the number he had dialled, he cursed loudly, and then noticing me, said, 'Who are you?' I briefly explained, and said I was waiting for the manager. 'Oh, that idiot. We call him the idiot here. Everyone does. Ask him.' Another man came in, powerfully built, expensively dressed and wearing a prominent necklace. 'This is a doctor, waiting for the idiot', he said, pointing at me. 'I don't know where he is', said the second, 'and I don't care either. What are you doing here?' I again briefly explained. 'There isn't a meeting today. There usually is, but it's been cancelled.' I began to feel uncomfortable and anxious, thinking I had mistaken the arrangements, and not sure who my two companions in the staff room were.

Steve appeared, a middle-aged man with a calming demeanour, and introduced himself to me, and the disrespect of my companions increased. 'I told this bloke that we call you the idiot', said the first, 'He's a psychiatrist, he must have come to see you, you're the mad one around here.' Steve ignored this, apologised that the meeting was starting late, led me in and introduced me to the seven or eight residents who were sitting around. During the meeting, Steve was continuously heckled, and it became clear that he interpreted the abuse as friendly teasing repartee, although I wondered if this ran a bit thin. At one point, he was challenged to tell me about his 'breasts'. He patiently explained that the residents were dependent on the hostel and the staff like a baby was dependent on its mother's breast. At times residents 'bit' the staff and himself like a baby bites the breast. The hecklers responded with riotous laughter and further taunting. When my moment on the agenda came, again the joke was made about how I must be there to assess Steve, to which he responded by suggesting that by the end of the project I might have something to report back about the hostel that would be helpful. Residents were broadly disinterested, and it seemed as though the presentation to them

was merely ritualistic. However, with prompting from Steve, I was asked some
sensible and searching questions about my role as an observer, and appro-
priate unease was expressed by residents about being watched. There seemed
to be broad agreement or acquiescence to my request, but I left the meeting
not entirely sure of the outcome.

I wrote to the residents' chairman to confirm my understanding that my
request was being granted, and proposed a time that I would visit weekly,
and a date for my first visit. I wrote that unless I heard to the contrary, I
would presume that this was OK.

The observations were arranged to start the following term, which
allowed several weeks to reflect on the experiences so far. I wondered
whether the rather anarchic and alarming tenor of the residents' meeting
could be understood as demonstrating therapeutic community principles
(Rapoport 1960). The manager refers me to the residents' meeting to
discuss my proposal, implying democratisation; he clearly tolerated considerable degrees of disturbance, and the residents' freedom with him
demonstrates the flattening of the hierarchy. Nevertheless, the damage that
had been done to the entrance door, and my own feeling of intimidation,
made me begin to wonder whether the therapeutic milieu was sufficiently
structured to contain the residents' disturbance.

THE OBSERVATIONS: TRANQUILLITY VERSUS MADNESS AND CRUELTY

After the dramatic and thought-provoking process of setting up the project,
my first few visits, and indeed the majority of the observations, were
characterised by monotony and boredom. In the central dining/television
room, usually two or three people sat around watching the television, with
no interaction between them for the hour. The monotony was broken by
someone entering or leaving, the television programme changing, or a
request to the pool players to be quiet. The quality of this monotony was
quite singular and characteristic, and yet difficult to define. Considerable
time was spent in my supervision seminar exploring it. My initial superficial
reaction was that it was relaxing and a welcome period for quiet reflection.
After a busy day, there seemed to be something tranquil about the hour's
observation. I just blended into the background: no one noticed me or
challenged me, I came in, sat down, then left about an hour later. No
demands were made on me, and I was left to just sit and watch – very
different to my previous experience of an infant observation project which
had been quite tense. The only problem was that here it felt as if there
wasn't much to see, or much of substance to take along to think about or
discuss in supervision. At the time, this seemed a genuine problem. Sitting

writing up the experience afterwards, I would look at the blank sheet of paper and not know what to say. In retrospect, the very lack of substance should have been remarkable – like the dramatic tension rises as banalities are shown in a play or film when you know that something of substance is around the corner.

The nature of the tranquillity was itself difficult to describe. It seemed timeless and still, like sitting in an empty church, or a place where one is accustomed to bustle and debate. Indeed it was rather like the experience of walking round the recently decanted wards in the large asylums which had been such hives of activity, and the centre of people's lives, but which are now unnaturally still. I was vaguely aware that there was something odd about this tranquillity, especially given the anarchic residents' meeting that I had attended. In the residents' meeting, it had occurred to me that I might become the focus of challenge similar to that tolerated by the manager, and that this might be potentiated by my role as observer. A paranoid resident group, not only having phantasies or delusions of being observed, but actually being observed and freed to challenge by the flattened hierarchy of the hostel's culture, seemed rather a frightening prospect. Instead, I found myself increasingly irritated by the weekly voyeurism of Oprah Winfrey and the patronising quiz game show that followed it. People living relatively normal lives putting themselves forward to exhibitionistically display the skeletons in their psychic or family cupboards, or displaying the highs and lows of winning or losing prizes on the basis of trivial questions irritated me increasingly. Putting the irritation together with the sense of expectant or unnatural tranquillity, I reflected that this irritation might be a symptom of an underlying anxiety about the calm exterior being a thin veneer over the livid emotional colour that had been evident in the meetings preceding it.

There was a pool table in the room which was occasionally used.

On the fifth visit, the room was quite full: there were about twelve people that I could see, four engaged in a game of pool, with two playing and two giving advice. Six or so were watching the television, and one or two could be seen in the kitchen preparing food which they individually brought in and ate. Others were munching their way through packets of chocolate digestive biscuits, and the tables and floor were strewn with empty packets and used plates. The repartee amongst the players was boisterous at times, and at one point I flinched as a mock threatening gesture was exchanged. Becoming aware that I was quite anxious, I observed feeling outnumbered, overwhelmed, and unable to maintain concentration on the several different foci of activity.

Evidence seemed to be added to the hypothesis that the monotony and tranquillity of the first four observational sessions was a thin skin covering more disturbing material.

The game of pool finished, and three of the four drifted off, leaving one hitting balls around the table on his own. Someone came through the door and asked him where one of the pool players had gone. 'Don't know,' he replied, 'don't know who he is. I thought he was your friend.' 'No, I don't know him', said the inquisitor 'I just wanted to give him a game.'

It was striking that this group of pool players who I had assumed to be intimates had strangers among them who blended in without difficulty as if no one noticed or cared. It clarified the way that I was received: in spite of looking out of place in a jacket and tie, in spite of obviously being a stranger, I just blended in, not noticeable amongst the comings and goings of people with food and other things to do.

On the seventh visit, the room was empty except for two people sitting together. It became clear that one was a staff member, as he acknowledged my appearance and introduced himself, then returned his attention to the television. After half an hour or so, the other man got up and began to pace around in an exaggerated manner, taking long slow deliberate steps. 'Aren't you tired,' the staff member said, 'after all, you were up all night. Do you want to go for a sleep?' The resident said nothing, but stopped in the middle of the room and lifted up his arms, adopting a pose which reminded me of pictures of the crucifixion of Christ. By this time, the staff member had sat forward, the television forgotten, anxiously watching his ward who remained stock still for ten minutes or so before slowly moving to another seat where he adopted another position, curled up this time. The staff member relaxed. Over this time several people had passed through, or fixed themselves something to eat, apparently oblivious to the drama in the room.

These observations made me wonder about the very tolerant and *laissez-faire* atmosphere in the hostel. I had seen toleration of the ridicule of staff by residents; toleration of strangers in its midst without comment, and toleration of extreme mental disorder. My discomfort that such licence might lead to anarchy was partly confirmed over the next few sessions.

In session nine, when I arrived, one of the residents, a slow heavy man, had lost his jacket. None of the six or seven people in the room had seen it. Several times over a 15-minute period he wandered in, looking behind chairs and in cupboards. 'Maybe it's been put out there in the bin', said another large man who I remembered had worn a necklace the day I had attended the meeting. He was stretched out on one of the sofas smoking, and pointed outside to a large dirty looking skip in the yard, visible from the room. In a dejected way, the searcher went outside to look, craning over the side of the skip. Another television watcher, the man with the crew-cut hair who had also been in the residents' meeting, then giggled and said, 'Is that where you put it?' 'No, I didn't hide it, you hid it' (with a laugh). 'Where did you put it?' The searcher returned, glowering now, and continued looking. 'What's wrong with your face?', demanded the man with the crew-cut, 'the bin's where it belongs anyway; its a disgusting jacket. You should chuck it away.' Saying this he threateningly got up and went over to where the searcher was now looking in another cupboard, as if provoking him. The searcher didn't answer back, but continued what he was doing, leaving the room shortly after.

After ten more minutes, the man with the crew-cut addressed another of the television watchers. 'What have you been doing today, Alf? Sitting on your fat arse, I suppose.' Another watcher responded, 'Alf, what d'you say we take him outside and give him a kicking. That'd teach him.' Instantly, the crew-cut had launched himself across the furniture to the man speaking; had put his head in an arm lock and was rubbing his knuckles into the unfortunate challenger's scalp. 'Don't you ever open your mouth again', he said, tightening his grip. 'What did I say?' Breathlessly, the challenger choked out the words, 'I won't, I won't.' 'NO!', shouted the crew-cut, 'Shut up, I said to keep your mouth shut.' After a few more moments (possibly long enough for the double-bind imposed by the crew-cut to sink in), the head lock was released, and order was restored. But after a few minutes, 'What did I tell you? What did I say?', the crew-cut taunted the challenger again. 'To keep my mouth . . .' 'SHUT UP!', yelled the crew-cut. This abusive catechism was repeated a few more times until the large man on the sofa told him to stop.

This observational session was extremely disturbing. I felt I was witness to abusive bullying and assault. Worse, I was colluding in the humiliation of the searcher by my inaction to either retrieve his coat or challenge the crew-cut; and I was guilty of collusion in the physical assault of the challenger by my doing nothing to intervene. The question plagued me: why had I done nothing? The obvious point was that it was not my role as a psychodynamic observer, but this seemed unsatisfactory. I had seen the crew cut and the large man on the couch in action in the residents' meeting, and briefly been challenged by them in the staff room preceding it. I was tolerated by them. I was accepted by them and would not be threatened, provided I didn't cross them. I was in cahoots, I was accepted by the gang for as long as I went along with it. It felt as though I was responsible for a total dereliction of my medical duty of care; that my inaction had been quite negligent.

I wondered if the staff group might feel as powerless as me in the face of these tyrannical dynamics, so that the toleration was partly imposed on them rather than being facilitated by them. By the eleventh session it had become clear that the bonhomie round the pool table covered quite naked struggles for power and supremacy, and occasionally staff were involved in playing. Several times, on previous visits, I had seen female staff playing, who had been trounced by the residents with genuine triumph.

In session eleven, a male member of staff was playing a series of games, and he clearly was a match for his opponents. He played two long and tense games watched by five or six residents, the television forgotten. In the first, the opponents had both cleared most of their balls, and the endgame was beginning. As the staff member lined up to play his shot, he was intentionally (if playfully) put off by a shout, mishit the cue ball and lost a shot. He protested, but in vain; there was a chorus of not very friendly quoting of the rules, and the penalty stood. His opponent potted his remainders and, with the black, won the game. The resident took full honours for winning, apparently oblivious of the unfair advantage that he had gained.

A little later, the same member of staff was on the table again, with the same air of tension apparent. The staff member played well, perhaps spurred on by his recent injustice. There was a grim silence among the five or six people watching as the extent of his lead became clear. He simply had the black to pot, and the resident lagged far behind. He was clearly going to win. As the resident played his shot, the staff member remembered that he had a phone call to make. Out he went into the staff room. The resident took his shot, and waited for the staff member to return. He waited and waited. Five minutes passed, the spectators drifted away, and the resident potted the rest of his balls and the black in a desultory way. Everyone seemed to have lost interest, leaving the room or slumping down in front of the television. About fifteen minutes after leaving the room, the staff member rushed through, apparently terribly preoccupied and busy. No one noticed.

It seemed as though the staff member's potency could not be tolerated, and had to be destroyed (in the first game he was about to win) by unfair means. In the second game, the staff member's potency seemed undeniable; he was clearly going to win even with further foul play. But he is unable to follow through, effectively abandoning the game. I wondered whether he had got the intimidatory message, and had substituted a structure of potency for a *laissez-faire* disavowal of authority.

In the twelfth and final observation session, I sat with three residents watching the television for an hour. Reflecting later, I think I relished the monotony of the television programmes as respite. I think that it is significant that I didn't seem to be observing the residents watching the television, but watched it with them. I was more interested in who won the toaster on the game show than I was in my surroundings. I wonder if, frankly, I didn't want to know about my surroundings, and what might emerge from them. My impression at the beginning of the project of tranquil calm seemed to make more sense. It reflected a resistance to seeing anything else beyond the illusion of tranquillity, forced by a fear of what might be unleashed or revealed by scratching the surface.

DISCUSSION

In broad terms, as the observation progressed, I moved from a perspective of seeing the culture in the hostel as tolerant and *laissez-faire* to becoming aware of a rather more disturbing dimension. The catatonic psychotic resident is not prescribed bed rest, hospitalisation or medication, but is followed, contained and tolerated to the extent that in spite of his disturbance he retains autonomy within the bounds of safety. The staff member tolerates the cheating in the pool game that makes him lose rather than assuming rank or staff superiority and delivering a lecture on the importance of fair play for mental health. Indeed the air of tolerance extends to people coming and going, playing pool or observing in a *laissez-faire* manner. The long observation sessions, where nothing happened except passage of the daytime TV programmes, had a tranquillity about them; a sort of timelessness, total structurelessness. In these observation sessions, I hypothesised that this *laissez-faire* tolerance might be therapeutic, and might be the ingredient of non-industrial cultures that is protective for schizophrenics: low expressed emotion, peace, calm and acceptance. It seemed as though on purpose, a social structure with staff and residents had been dismantled so that clients were not stressed by being unable to conform to them. In a vacuum of social structure, whatever you do, whatever you are, or whatever you believe, is OK.

This impression of a social structural vacuum, however, is deceptive. Nature abhors a vacuum, and the social vacuum left by the deconstruction of the medical social framework of the psychiatric ward is filled with an autocratic, hegemonic alternative. The manager's 'stupidity' is not tolerated; his explanations about dependency are not tolerated, and, in my preparatory visit, they are contemptuously ridiculed in front of a professional visitor. The basic human rights of respect and property ownership of the man who loses his jacket are violated in a sadistic and cruel attack by the crew-cut, who hides the jacket and sends him on fruitless ventures to find it. The challenger is assaulted and battered, his physical autonomy violated, and the social structure is so rigid that there is nothing he can do. The rigidity and totality is illustrated by the double bind that the challenger is put in. If he speaks, he is verbally assaulted; if he is silent, he is verbally assaulted.

It seemed as though into the vacuum of social structure had rushed an alternative: a pecking order; a 'might is right' ideology; an authority structure based on fear and intimidation rather than on professional roles and responsibilities. This process has been described both in literature and in academic theory. In Golding's *Lord of the Flies* (1954), a group of public school boys are marooned on an island, isolated from the hierarchical social structure of the school. In its place something worse emerges, far more oppressive and destructive than school rules. Similarly, in Orwell's *Animal Farm* (1945), an initial *laissez-faire* co-operative between the farmyard animals becomes colonised by a new and more ruthless autocracy run by the pigs, making the initial regime look like a benign paternalism. Freud's (1921) model of the 'Primal Horde' follows the development in groups where a leader with absolute authority (and sole access to all the females) emerges from an unorganised group.

Closer to the specific situation in the mental health hostel, Barron (1987) described the unravelling of a day hospital which was run along therapeutic community lines. She describes the adoption of a psychoanalytic authority structure in place of the traditional medical or psychiatrically oriented one. This new structure was based on two things. Firstly, 'free' association which led to an ideology of permissiveness and introduced an extreme *laissez-faire* attitude which effectively dismantled the structure. Secondly, into this vacuum an alternative authority and power structure grew – one based on access to or understanding of the unconscious. Unlike a more standard medical authority structure which has its checks and balances, the new one had no appeals or complaints procedure. Protest was understood as resistance; disagreement and objections were dismissed as the individual's psychopathology to create an utterly unimpeachable and hegemonic structure where power was held by those with perceived psychodynamic depth of insight. Meals and travel passes were declared enactments of dependency, and were stopped. Unable to negotiate within the day hospital, patients complained to the Local Authority, leading to an enquiry, questions in the House of Commons, and eventually closure.

The most important dimension in which to speculate about the effect of the environment is that of the internal world because, quintessentially, mental health problems are disorders of this arena. In supervision, some of the effects of the environment on me (as the observer) were explored. Exploring and debating my own reactions in the supervisory setting distilled out two main themes: firstly, the sense of menace at violence not far beneath the surface calm; secondly, the impression of a lack of containment. The contrast between the calm and the violence was quite startling; the observation seemed to see-saw between extremes of violence and psychological terrorism to utter calm and acceptance. The impression of violence not far beneath the surface was presumably behind my flinching while the pool players exchanged banter. One possibility mooted was that in some way the calm and the violence were linked. The staff member refrains from winning the game of pool because it might cause a ripple in the calm pond of the organisation; the sense of menace enforces the calm, residents are too frightened to cause any trouble. In session nine, in between the humiliation of the searcher and the assault on the challenger, the sense of calm and monotony was there as people returned their attention to the TV; this in spite of what had just taken place.

The lack of containment issue runs through the observation. On my first visit, no one knows who I am or why I'm there; the person I'm due to meet is off sick, but the meeting is neither cancelled nor added to someone else's diary. My own anxiety was derived from being a new visitor, and at crossing something of a cultural boundary (a doctor in a non-medical and even anti-psychiatric establishment). Some of this anxiety might have been contained by the staff group by being mindful of my visit, but it was not. Psychosis can be conceived of as a failure of mental structure; the ego is overwhelmed by phantasies, anxieties and unconscious contents which it fails to distinguish from reality. I had evolved a view that for containment and treatment, people with psychotic disorders need structure; that they needed unambivalent boundaries and clarity. This need seemed to me to explain why medical practice in mental health is replete with this sort of structure: hard theories of mental illness and brain biochemistry; a hard legal framework in the Mental Health Act and the firm social medical hierarchy described. The ethos of the hostel deconstructs these frameworks which contain people's psychotic problems. As well as the concrete and social deconstruction previously mentioned, there is the psychological defensive deconstruction of the psychodynamic approach and the deconstruction of the pathologisation of mental experiences invoked by the social model.

Discussion in supervision of the material in the seventh visit, where the psychotic man adopted the posture of Christ, threw up an interesting observation. In this session I was aware of feeling much less anxious. It seemed as though being able to make a psychiatric diagnosis had provided me with an identity; I could be a psychiatrist. Having an internal structure (identity as a psychiatrist) reduced the anxiety created in the absence of legitimised social structure in the hostel. This seemed to demonstrate the interplay between structure in the internal and external worlds, for myself at least as the observer, and so the significance of Rosenfeld's work fell into place. Rosenfeld's (1971) account of the way that a fragmented mind ruthlessly maintains intra-psychic order amongst internal objects like a Mafia gang seemed to be a description of aspects of the hostel's environment. Stability is maintained but at the expense of creativity and growth; freedom is restricted because the internal mafia insists on the maintenance of self-damaging symptoms and attitudes.

Perhaps the internal effect of the dissolution of the more traditional medical model psychiatric structure was a sort of identity crisis, where the purpose and place of the individual is undefined. The question arose as to how the residents dealt with this sense of identity diffusion. Perhaps the man looking for his coat is more comfortable doing this, because it gives him a purpose and a role. Perhaps residents collude with the tyrannical social order because being at the bottom of the pecking order is better than being adrift with no references whatsoever. Most interesting was the catatonic man's symptom seen as a reaction to the culture. In standard psychiatric practice, catatonia is relatively rare these days; indeed the man in the hostel was only the second I had seen in five years of psychiatry. Was his need to hold himself in a particular place and posture a response to an environment in which his 'place' was completely undefined? In his psychosis, did he become Christ (a rather overwhelming identity) in response to his own identity being dissolved away? Did crucifixion represent a strong and undeniable role (dying for the sins of the world) or did it represent a slow mental death, unable to move because of terror of Rosenfeldian Mafia reprisals? Residents are unable to tolerate freedom in the physical and social environments and substitute this with rigid room usage and a tyrannical hegemony. Maybe this man was unable to tolerate acceptance and toleration of his inner world and had to develop a movement disorder (his catatonia) to put a physical structure around his mind.

The theme running through the observations and discussions in supervision concerned the dialectic between structure and non-structure. This hostel, and the social mental health movement in general, has a critique of medical model psychiatry that it is too structured; the idea that in structure imposed by the medical model of diagnosis and treatment, and the power relation between physician and patient, there is insufficient freedom for the humanity of the patient or the person to emerge. This structured approach to mental health reaches its apogee in the management of the long-term mentally ill in large bureaucratic hospital settings. There, structure is everything, patients have a place in the physical structure of the hospital, a bed and a bedside cupboard in a ward. They have a place in the asylum social structure: at the bottom of a hierarchy, with the doctor at the top and the nurse in the middle. Their experiences in their inner world have a structure: they are 'delusions' or 'hallucinations' in a structure of phenomenology which fits neatly into a taxonomic and diagnostic structure. People do not have disturbing feelings and things happen to them: they have symptoms of schizophrenia, manic depression, and so on.

In the hostel, there is a clear move to remove or renegotiate these structures. Physically, the building is part of the community, residents shop locally, visit the local GP and other services; they cook for themselves and are to a large degree physically autonomous. The open plan large central room expresses this concretely. Sitting in this room I could observe activities from gaming through social activities, cooking, eating, negotiation with staff, and so on. However, into this architectural expression of freedom, constraints and limitations are imposed. A straitjacket of daytime TV and an unwritten code that watching it was the room's primary function.

By the end of the project, it seemed to me that the abusive tyranny that had developed in the hostel is a function of the extreme need for the containment and structure of people with psychotic disorders. This raises the corollary that the apparent abusiveness of the back wards in the large mental hospitals is effect rather than cause in exactly the same way. If this is true, then the 'back ward' culture may have evolved to be containing and may have evolved in response to their needs. How, then, does the observer of the back ward conceptualise the unbearability of life there? Perhaps what is unbearable is not the environment, be it hospital ward, community hostel or shop doorway in a large city where people seek out an existence on the streets; perhaps what is unbearable is the internal world of the person with a severe mental disorder. Perhaps any setting that tries to contain the severely mentally ill will start to reflect this unbearability.

CONCLUSION

This observation project used the psychodynamic observational methodology developed by Hinshelwood to examine the culture and environment of a community mental health hostel for psychiatric patients. I feel that my initial hypothesis was rather confirmed; namely, that the unbearability of structures set up to contain the severely mentally ill derived from the unbearability of mental illness, rather than from the structures *per se*.

It is clear that there are considerable differences between this and the psychiatric hospital long-stay back ward. In a hospital, there are clear structures which govern and regulate the concrete environment, the social environment and the internal world. The back ward is in a hospital, a community apart often with a wall round it; the social structure is a medical hierarchy with power allocated to doctors and nurses. The experiences of the internal world are deemed to be psychopathology; delusions and hallucinations which are modified with drugs and ECT. This over-structuralisation can be dehumanising and traumatic to patients who are given a label of mental illness and assigned the role of mental patient.

On the surface, it would seem as though the alternative available in the hostel is far more beneficial and therapeutic; a homely and friendly environment in the local community where former patients can live together with unobtrusive and low key supervision by staff. The problem is that this easy going environment with little in the way of authority or other structures presents people with a different set of problems. Where do they fit into this amorphous organisation; what is their role; what is the meaning of their mental experiences? To fill the structural vacuum, other structures, hierarchies and attitudes develop which may be more damaging than those that they replace.

   Both the mental hospital ward and the community hostel attempt in different ways to contain severe mental disturbance, but neither can obviate the distress and unbearability that is severe mental illness. There is a risk that reformers will mistakenly conclude that the distress and unbearability that they perceive in such settings is a function of the regime rather than the nature of the beast. Consequently, they may devise new approaches that will be more damaging in the long run to those they are trying to help.

Part III

Observations in general health care

Chapter 8

Working in a world of bodies

A medical ward

Wilhelm Skogstad

INTRODUCTION

In their daily work with physically ill patients nurses face many difficult and conflictual feelings. They encounter illness and death all the time and in their direct contact with the bodies of patients are also confronted with the sexuality that these bodies represent. This arouses deep anxieties and conflicts in the individuals working with the patients, and these are often felt as too difficult to experience and think about. A particular culture develops on a ward in which these anxieties and conflicts are defended against. The culture is characterised by a set of certain defensive techniques that staff use both individually and collectively.

This study is based on a weekly observation of a medical ward over a period of four months. The observation method itself is described in detail in Chapter 2. It investigates the culture of this ward and looks at the defensive techniques that were used to ward off the anxieties and mental pain that working with physically ill people and with their bodies and emotions entailed. Although one could see in individual staff members an ability to think about the feelings aroused, the general culture of the ward was characterised by strong defences against those feelings. Of particular importance were manic excitement and erotisation and defences of a bodily and concrete nature.

WORKING WITH BODIES AND FEELINGS

Nurses who work with physically ill patients are constantly faced with severe and often life threatening physical illness and with death. They have to struggle in themselves, consciously or unconsciously, with their anxieties about illness, death and dying, with their fear of loss and their feelings of guilt. They face anxieties about their capacity to care for others and keep them alive and are often confronted with feelings of helplessness.

Apart from their own individual painful feelings, the nurses are also subjected to the anxiety, depression, envy, helplessness and fury of the patients and of their relatives. Patients and relatives often feel extremely disturbed by the illness and search for containers into which they can project their distress.

The daily work of the nurses involves a close contact with the patients' bodies, which itself arouses anxieties. The physical contact is often of a closeness and a kind similar to the relationship of a mother and an infant. Touching, feeding and washing, even dealing with excrement, are common. This revives infantile wishes and anxieties of one's early mother–infant relationship, oedipal phantasies and fears as well as sexual wishes of a more adult kind which cause anxieties and conflicts.

I observed a medical ward which specialised in cardiological diseases but had in fact a wide range of illnesses. In heart conditions very sudden deaths can occur, a patient's condition may suddenly change dramatically and need quick and efficient care or even resuscitation. The fear of sudden and unexpected death, and the anxiety of not being able to keep someone alive, is stirred by such work. Feelings of guilt if a patient doesn't survive or deteriorates are fairly common, as are doubts about one's competence. On the other hand, cardiological patients can make remarkable recoveries, and nurses and doctors experience successes which may reassure them but also tempt them to feel omnipotent.

The pressure of the new NHS system, with its scarceness of resources and emphasis on cost-effectiveness, leads to additional difficulties and anxieties. Working with a shortage of staff and under the constant pressure of performance checks and audits, financial considerations and job insecurity, can stretch people to their limits.

The work of nurses with physically ill patients happens to a large extent on a physical level, with the patients' bodies. However, attending to the bodies can in itself be used defensively to avoid the conflicts that relating to whole persons brings about; this was so on the ward I observed. During the course of my observations I increasingly had the impression that the work with bodies also led to a particular set of bodily and concrete defences and attitudes on this ward: the body was used both to communicate and to defend, and concrete ways of defending against anxieties and mental pain were commonly used, instead of symbolic ones.

ANXIETIES AND SOCIAL DEFENCES

In all social institutions, the specific area of work brings up anxieties and conflicts that have to be dealt with by developing particular ways of coping with these anxieties. Individual defences come together to form a culture of defensive techniques that in turn influence the functioning of the individuals in the institution. These social defences are necessary to a degree but can also become so rigid and gross that they impair the ability of the individuals to fulfil the tasks they are there to perform. Such a psychoanalytical model of institutions and some of the relevant literature are discussed in more detail in Chapter 1. In this chapter, therefore, the literature most relevant to this particular study is referred to only briefly.

Menzies' ([1959] 1988) well-known original study was carried out in a general hospital, too, and was therefore also about the work with bodies, physical illness and death. She pointed particularly to the strong and contrasting feelings that this work stirred up in the nurses: of pity and love, guilt and anxiety, hatred, resentment and envy of the care patients receive. She also emphasised the strong libidinal and erotic impulses which were brought up by the close contact with bodies, and caused anxiety. Cohn (1994), in a work with a special care unit for babies, noted the deep anxieties in staff about their capacity to keep the babies alive, which were also observed by Fletcher (1983). Roberts (1994a) described how staff in a hospital for the long-term care of elderly people were faced with anxieties about ageing, being useless and rejected. And Ramsay (Chapter 10) showed staff's deep anxieties in the face of death.

These authors all found that the anxieties they described were dealt with by the development of strongly defensive cultures which aimed at evading rather than modifying these anxieties. In Menzies' general hospital, for example, this was done through a splitting-up of the nurse–patient relationship, by detachment and anonymisation; in Cohn's special care unit for babies, through a kind of mechanical care that did everything but without emotional care; and in Ramsay's hospice, the experience of death was shut out and isolated.

THE HOSPITAL AND THE WARD

The hospital in which I carried out the observation was a medium-sized general hospital outside of London. Each of its medical wards had an emphasis on certain specialties which had been introduced to the wards, not only to improve the care of patients but to increase the satisfaction of the nurses. The introduction of the internal market had influenced the hospital greatly and, with pride, the lead nurse told me in my initial meeting that the nurses were now involved in the business side. However, I also sensed that this put an enormous pressure on staff, poignantly reflected in her comment that if they didn't break even there wouldn't be the money to pay their salaries.

The ward I observed was specialised in cardiology, but not restricted to heart diseases. For certain investigations like angiography patients had to be transferred to another, bigger hospital. My initial discussion with the lead nurse gave me an impression of a general sense of inferiority in relation to this bigger, more renowned hospital. In this initial contact I was also struck by the friendly, welcoming atmosphere which, however, somehow felt too quickly welcoming. Doubts and critical questions about myself and the aim of my project only came up later in discussion. Then the Lead Nurse expressed the worry that I would write something critical in the *British Medical Journal*, and would say that the nurses were 'doing a terrible job'. In this way she expressed the nurses' self-doubts as well as their persecutory fears (which may have had a realistic basis in the climate they were working in).

STARTING THE OBSERVATION

The observation involved a visit to the ward once a week for an hour at the same time, and I always sat in the same place. Before I started these regular visits, I introduced myself in a ward staff meeting and explained my project to the nurses. In the same meeting a woman counsellor who was offering staff support groups in the hospital introduced herself as well. When this offer was discussed, the nurses emphasised the pressure and stress they were experiencing, but also conveyed that their way of dealing with the strain was to smoke, forget or have a rest. There was a sense of great neediness, for example when they asked the counsellor for individual instead of only group sessions. This sense of neediness also came up later when they joked to me that I could sit at the desk and answer the phone when I came for my observations. The counsellor tried to think with them how best to set up a support group, and encouraged them to think about it and get back to her. However, she was quickly overruled by a firm decision of the ward sister to have two groups for different nurse grades and to start one group the following week.

This beginning was quite telling. Not only was a lot of strain, anxiety and need expressed in this staff meeting, but the nurses were actually given the chance of a mental space for exploring their strains and feelings. The response to it was a great pressure to avoid thinking and feeling and to find a way out by an instant action – in this case through a quick decision that wasn't thought through. I think that the same tendency was behind their joking suggestion that I could help them, as if my action would solve their problem. I think the nurses feared that giving mental space to their experiences would lead to painful feelings that were too difficult to bear. Therefore such space couldn't be allowed, and a problem had to be' solved' or, rather, got rid of instantly without proper thinking or feeling.

FLEETING FRIENDLINESS: OUT OF SIGHT, OUT OF MIND

There was usually a friendly and pleasant, yet somehow superficial, atmosphere on the ward. Patients and relatives were treated in a jolly, sometimes warm and considerate, but more often slightly joking way – as I was. Staff usually greeted me with a friendly smile and on a few occasions I was encouraged to get a coffee from the kitchen or offered some chocolate. However, the friendly contact was usually quite superficial and fleeting and the staff showed a quick succession of engaging and disengaging. In this way, any sense of real loss, for example, was dealt with by being pushed out of their minds with great speed.

In my first observation I see an older woman who is leaving the ward, accompanied by her daughter. The staff nurse Trudy has a friendly chat with her and jokes to her about 'Hotel Redwood Hospital', conveying some pride in the way they provide for patients. Then the nurse and the patient embrace each other and stand for a while in the corridor with their arms around each other until the patient leaves with her daughter. The nurse goes on to do other things, appearing as efficient as in any other moment before or after. Later, another woman patient is leaving. A nurse, Esther, says goodbye to her in a warm and friendly way, and Trudy jokes that the patient should pay the man who will push her outside in a wheelchair (he is in fact a hospital staff member responsible for transporting patients). A moment later when the patient again says ''Bye' to Esther while being pushed out of the ward, the nurse returns the ''Bye' in a cool and distant way as if there has never been any contact between the two.

The friendliness of these goodbyes, one even including a more intimate bodily contact, was quite striking. But equally striking was the speed with which the patients then appeared gone, so that a moment after an apparently intimate exchange the nurse Trudy looked completely unmoved and Esther treated the other like a stranger. The nurses seemed capable of quickly engaging in an apparently close contact and quickly detaching themselves again. Some deeper resentment of the patients' demands was hidden in Trudy's jokes. Although the nurses seemed able to make a friendly and humane contact, the experience of sorrow and loss which real contact would bring up was prevented by this superficial and fleeting contact and the speedy shift of attaching and detaching themselves. Donati (Chapter 3) has described as 'touch and go' the encounters of staff and patients on a chronic psychiatric ward which were quickly broken off. The encounters she described, however, lacked the liveliness that was characteristic of the ward I observed.

The ability of the nurses on this ward to rid their minds of any memory in order to avoid a sense of loss is also illustrated by two small vignettes:

In one observation, a few nurses are sitting together, having some time to chat, and one of the nurses, Jane, gets a plastic bag with chocolate and biscuits and a card in it – a present from a patient. She can't remember the name of the patient and has to look in the card.

In another observation the telephone rings, and a nurse, Andrew, answers. He asks the person to wait and goes to the board with all the names of patients on it but cannot find the name he is looking for. Then he searches for another nurse who is able to tell him that the patient is still on the ward but is being discharged that day.

The names of the patients who had left were quickly wiped off the board, seemingly not just in the physical space (the board) but equally in the mental space (the memory), and were replaced by new ones. This seemed to be their way of dealing with the constant changes of patients: attending to the ones who were there and quickly wiping out any awareness of the others. Such techniques helped them not to be overburdened by thoughts and feelings about all those patients and relationships and not to experience a recurrent sense of loss.

I often had the sense that any contact needed to be restricted to a brief encounter, no matter whether the nurses were under pressure or would have had sufficient time.

A student nurse, on a quiet day, having nothing in particular to do at that moment, starts a conversation with a patient who is lying in her bed but is called away by the ward sister to do a particular task. Half an hour later he strolls again into the bay that I can look into, appearing as if he is just about to start another conversation with a different patient, but before he can he is called again and told to do a blood sugar stick, even though he had been asked before to do that at a later time.

I felt a deep disappointment when the nurse had to rush away again. In my lonely observing position I empathised with the patient's need for human contact. Although there were many cheerful encounters, they were usually brief and observations like this one suggested that there was an active preventing of a more ordinary, humane and potentially more emotional conversation.

In my observations I could see the nurses' attempts to form friendly and humane relationships in which they could experience themselves as caring and attached to their patients. But I could also see their strong tendency to show a superficial, at times almost manic kind of friendliness while distancing themselves from any deeper human contact. Becoming more attached to patients also meant getting closer to experiencing more painful feelings like pity, guilt, anxiety and loss, but also resentment, and this made them feel the need to protect themselves by cutting off their feelings and wiping out memories.

SEEING AND TURNING AWAY

I could often see evidence of the conflict between providing an adequate mental space and turning away to avoid feeling overwhelmed and pained. The following vignettes give examples both of a more open, less-defended contact and of a much more defensive avoidance of any real contact.

It is quite rushed on the ward. A man of about fifty arrives and nurse Trudy speaks to him in the corridor, asking him whether he is aware of what is going on with his mother. The man talks about a broken hip, some heart problems and some other things. Trudy then says that they should probably have a private place to talk. I feel concerned for this man as his mother is probably in a much more serious state than he thinks she is. Trudy looks into the staff room, which is occupied, then gets the key to the ward sister's office and goes there with him. After a few minutes she returns and later she makes a remark to a colleague that the man was very upset.

On another day it is again quite hectic on the ward. In the midst of other people, a nurse, Ann, says to a relative after clarifying which patient his mother is: 'I need to speak to you privately, there are so many people around.' A moment later, she starts speaking to him in the corridor, very close to me and another visitor. Then the monitor goes off, Ann goes to turn it off and returns, saying 'One day we will have a quiet conversation.' She tells the man about his mother, who is soon going to be discharged, and she suggests all sorts of help he should get, like a cleaning lady and Meals-on-Wheels. The man says a few times that he does these things himself and adds that he is not working now and that doing things for his mother keeps him occupied. Ann continues to emphasise that he should think about getting such help, until eventually the man says that he will. I feel uncomfortable being made to listen to this conversation and sorry for the man.

In both situations the nurse was aware of the need for a private space and attention. In the first example the space was actually provided, both physically and mentally. The relative was seen in a separate room, even though only briefly, and the nurse was thinking about his need and later his upset. Her thoughtful response was reflected in my own sense of concern. Quite differently, in the second example the nurse provided neither the physical nor the mental space. She realised the need for privacy but nevertheless talked to the man in public. Her response to his comments showed that she was not really able to think about his needs.

Instead of listening to him properly she filled him up with 'good advice', which to me did not feel helpful at all. Part of the reasons for handling the situation in this way was, I think, the enormous strain the nurse was under, experiencing demands from every direction. Her remark on returning from the monitor suggested that she felt guilty for not providing the privacy and mental space, but presumably this only increased her need to defend herself against feelings of concern, pity and guilt.

As common practice in this country, the ward was laid out in bays rather than rooms. Each bay had four beds, and if some privacy was needed a curtain was drawn around the bed. With this layout, any suffering could potentially be seen all the time by the nurses. To take in all the suffering, empathise with the patients and think about their needs, can easily feel too much. I think that the nurses experienced this often as a huge demand on them and felt resentful and guilty about it. In order to avoid this conflict, frequently they actively turned away from the suffering.

From my usual place of observation I could see one bed in the nearest bay without any restriction. In there I quite often observed a patient suffering physically or emotionally but very much on his or her own.

One day a woman patient in this bed is looking around with longing eyes. Then she looks at me with an expression of loneliness and a deep wish for contact. No one else seems to be aware of her need. I feel guilty and ashamed, unable to give her anything, and look away.

Another day a woman patient is sitting up in her bed with a bowl in front of her, trying with great difficulty to cough up. She is sweating and clearly suffering, but doesn't call anyone. At one point she looks at me and seems to feel ashamed that she is being seen. Meanwhile, Peter, a male nurse, is near the entrance of this bay, chatting with a young female doctor who puts her arm around his waist and then caresses his neck. I feel a mixture of guilt for not attending to this patient and anger with the nurse and the doctor.

As observer I showed the same movement which I could detect in staff, of seeing and then turning away. In the first vignette I had a sense of a great emotional demand on me, too great to fulfil, which left me feeling guilty and ashamed. I didn't even do what my observer role would have allowed, like smiling at her, thus acknowledging her as a person; instead I looked away. The way I turned my eyes and my mind away from the feeling of demand and guilt reflected the movement that was fairly common in the staff. The second vignette shows a grosser example of this. While *I* had the painful and conflictual feelings that staff could have had, *they* engaged in an erotic activity and ignored the patient's suffering. This public display of intimacy may have contributed to the patient's sense of shame about her suffering being seen.

FLIRTATIOUSNESS AND EROTIC ATMOSPHERE

Erotisation, as in the previous example, was quite a common social defence in this ward culture. The atmosphere was often flirtatious, and both verbal and physical contact between staff members frequently had an erotic quality. Nurses called each other 'Darling' and stroked each other. Nurse Peter often had long flirtatious chats with one of the female doctors, as in the previous example, or embraced her; he was also generally at the centre of the female junior doctors' erotic interest. I felt that there were two aspects to the erotic atmosphere. On the one hand it was an expression of the sexual feelings aroused by the close physical contact with patients. Expressing them in a fleeting, light and humorous way made them less frightening, and the atmosphere more pleasant and playful. On the other hand, the erotic atmosphere was a powerful defence against anxieties, particularly the fear of death.

A female patient calls a nurse because she needs to go to the toilet. The nurse, a handsome young black man, almost dances around her bed. Then he fetches the toilet chair in a playfully dramatic way which they both laugh about. He closes the curtains around her bed and leaves her. After a while he peeps in and laughs at her in a light and somewhat flirtatious way.

The situation between a woman and a young man around something as intimate as the toilet stirs up sexual phantasies, anxieties and embarrassment. This was dealt with by the nurse by turning it into a light, humorous and erotic interchange, thus making it easier for both of them.

The flirtatious or erotic atmosphere often came up when there was great pressure or a crisis – even after a death, as I will show later. Erotisation provided a playful way out of unbearable tension and a powerful defence against depressive feelings and anxieties. Doubts about their ability to keep patients alive, fears about death and a deep sense of guilt could be dealt with by creating an atmosphere of erotic playfulness, excitement and physical touching. The following example shows how initial tension and anxiety was turned into erotic excitement; later in this chapter I will show how the crisis after a death was dealt with in such a way.

In my fifth observation the atmosphere is initially very hectic. The monitor goes off frequently and the corridor seems full of relatives waiting to speak to a nurse. The transfer of five patients to other hospitals has to be organised, and

Nancy and Ann appear tense, not quite knowing how they will manage. Nancy makes a number of phone calls to sort this out, one of them to nurse Mary whom she asks whether she can come in early next morning to help, and she calls her 'Darling'. She makes some more phone calls in a high-pitched, sweet tone of voice, again saying 'Darling'. When Ann goes into one of the single rooms she says 'Darling' to a patient in a rather excited tone of voice. Eventually the problems are sorted out and the atmosphere becomes a little calmer.

Then a female junior doctor is standing at the desk, chatting flirtatiously with nurse Peter. The telephone rings, Peter answers and calls Nancy who comes to the phone. It appears to be a private call, and she arranges something for the next evening. While doing this, she strokes the doctor's soft jumper quite sensuously, clearly enjoying this. The doctor carries on chatting, unperturbed by this. Eventually Nancy makes a remark to her about the jumper. A bit later, Nancy has a conversation at the desk with Ann, who is sitting while she is standing. Nancy goes tenderly through Ann's hair with her hand and makes a remark about it. Suddenly Ann realises that I am watching them and says 'He's observing our conversation.'

On this day, the nurses were in a very difficult situation being bombarded by overwhelming demands. In this tense and anxious atmosphere there was a desperate attempt to make things more bearable by creating an erotic and excited interchange. Initially this was reflected in Nancy's tone of voice and the repetitive 'Darling', but after a while the atmosphere became highly erotic and flirtatious, and then all anxiety seemed to have disappeared. Now staff were engaged with each other in an excited relationship from which the patients and myself were excluded. I felt an outsider, jealous of their intimacy and pleasure. With this powerful defensive technique they were able to free themselves of all the tension and anxiety, becoming cheerful and excited instead, while the miserable feelings of exclusion, envy and despair were lodged in those around them – the patients and the observer. One of the nurses seemed to become aware of this state of affairs when she realised they were being observed and then felt a sense of guilt or shame.

MOVING BODIES

There was an enormous turnover and movement of patients on this ward. Some were discharged home, others were transferred to another hospital for cardiological investigations or operations, usually returning after a while. Often patients were also moved within the hospital to another ward to make space for new patients in this ward. In addition, patients were moved from one bay to another in the ward. New patients usually came into either of the first two bays and were moved further down the ward when they no longer needed monitoring. But even within the other bays patients were moved, sometimes to have an all-male or all-female bay, sometimes for no reason apparent to me. This meant that there was a constant break-up of relationships, between nurses and patients as well as between patients, and any familiar place was quickly lost again.

As observer I felt the impact of these changes. Each week the bay I could look into appeared different. I often wondered whether a patient I had seen the previous week was still there. If not, I felt a sense of disappointment and loss but also wondered whether they had died or recovered. Whenever I saw a familiar face I was pleased, and would often look at the board with the patients' names to find familiar ones. I always had a strong wish to be recognised by the nurses and was pleased and felt at home when I was. I also had strong feelings about 'my place', the place where I usually sat. If this was taken and I had to sit somewhere else, even though nearby, I felt estranged and displaced.

What I experienced in myself – the longing for contact and recognition, the sense of loss and abandonment, the wish to hold onto my physical place and the feeling of displacement if this was lost – reflected feelings that patients and nurses probably shared but often dared not think about or express. At times, nurses seemed able to be in touch with some of those feelings, but more often they turned to a defensive way of functioning.

In one of the calmer observations there seemed more space to think. Then I saw that nurses could be aware how difficult all the changes and losses were for themselves and for the patients (even though I never heard them question the practice of so much moving):

A patient needs to be moved within the ward, and Nancy is thinking with another nurse whom it might be best to move. She asks a patient whether he wants to go into one of the single rooms and accepts when he says 'No'. Later a patient is brought onto the ward and the nurse says to him 'Sorry about all the moving! Now you won't be moved again'.

In both these situations the nurse was in touch with the difficulty that moving meant for a person and took that into account, although in the second there was also some denial of the reality, as it seemed unrealistic on this ward to give a guarantee that a patient would not be moved again.

Under greater pressure, the atmosphere became more defensive. Then the acknowledgement of the emotional pain that movings and break-ups brought about was lost or projected into others.

One day, Trudy and another nurse are gathering in front of the bay because they need to move a patient to make space for a new one. When Jane comes, Trudy says: 'I'm so pleased you're here, we're already getting mad!' They go through all the patients and find various physical reasons why most of them cannot be moved. Trudy suggests a male patient and Jane says, 'His family will go mad!' They seem horrified at the potential reaction of the patient's family. Eventually they call the doctor and explain that this is the only patient they can move. Before Jane phones the family, she says to the other nurses: 'Well, wish me luck, ladies!' When she actually speaks to a member of the patient's family, in a friendly, but firm way, I get the sense that it is not a huge problem to convince them that the move is necessary.

On another day of great tension on the ward, a patient in a critical state needs to be admitted and staff try to identify another patient who can be discharged that afternoon. Eventually someone is found, an Asian man with broken English who is awaiting his angiography and whose medication seems not yet to be sufficiently sorted out. The registrar, who had been in obvious distress about the new patient, tells the Asian man that he has to leave in a tone as if it was most natural to be discharged so abruptly. However, the doctor seems to be perturbed by my observing presence and eventually asks me in a critical and hostile way who I am, what I'm doing, what my profession is. I feel extremely uncomfortable, but also get the sense that he feels threatened and persecuted by my observing.

In both cases the feelings about moving and discharging were too disturbing to be kept in the minds of the staff. If they empathised with the patients and thought properly about what they were doing to them, they would be faced with a painful sense of unease and guilt. These feelings were, therefore, projected outside into others. In the first example, it was the relatives who were seen as so 'mad' that one could hardly dare to contact them. I think this was a reflection of the strength of the staff's own feelings which were felt to be too dangerous to be got in contact with. The projection became quite evident in that the relatives did not react as expected. In the second example, the deep unease, as well as the persecutory guilt, was projected into me. Instead of the registrar having such feelings it was I who was made to feel uncomfortable and was experienced as a critical observer, like a harsh super-ego.

Apart from the discharges and transfers to other hospitals, I did not feel convinced that all these moves were really necessary and could not have been avoided if there had been the genuine wish not to move patients. A culture of constant moving had been created in which the impact of such changes on vulnerable, ill persons was to a large extent denied. The staff of the hospital lived to some degree in a world of bodies instead of a world of people with feelings.

USING THE BODY

The nursing work on a medical ward with physically ill patients obviously consists to a large extent in physical care, in attending to the patients' bodies. At least on this ward, the close and direct contact with the bodies had an enormous impact on the whole culture. For example, the body played an important part for the nurses when they were showing care and affection. This took the form of providing food and drink for each other as well as for me, of touching and caressing each other, or of holding and embracing a patient. The body often appeared to be the currency of this ward with which a lot could be expressed. The body was used, even if the main intention was about emotional care and support. The use of the body seemed to make things easier to tolerate, and was therefore used defensively. Remaining in a world of bodies, and expressing feelings on a bodily level, could spare the mind the burden of anxieties and conflicts in relation to whole persons.

There was often friendly contact between nurses and patients where the body was used to convey affection. Sometimes, however, this had an infantilising quality to it. Both aspects are illustrated in the following example:

When Nancy says goodbye to an older woman, who is just about to be pulled away in a wheelchair, she holds the woman's face between her hands for some time while speaking to her warmly. 'Look after yourself! Don't stop eating and drinking! Otherwise you will be back here again and we don't want that.' When the patient replies 'Yes, I don't want that either', Nancy says 'So look after yourself!' A bit later Nancy speaks to relatives of a patient who has just died on the ward. I can't hear what is being said but I can see her putting an arm around one of the relatives while speaking to them.

The body also played a large part in the contact of the nurses amongst each other and sometimes between nurses and doctors, not only in an erotic way, as described earlier, but also to convey affection.

On a particularly tense day, in the middle of hectic work, a younger nurse, Jane, leans on the chest of a taller and older nurse, Helen, with her head on Helen's breasts as if she wanted to cry there. It is only for a moment and then they part and continue doing their work.

On another day, the nurses Andrew and Judith are standing at the board. Judith sighs, says she is tired and talks about all the patients who are coming back from other hospitals or have to move somewhere else. She puts her arm around Andrew's waist and Andrew does the same with her. In this posture they stand in front of me for a while and then go off together, arm in arm, probably to have a coffee.

The impact of this world of bodies on the culture of the ward, however, went far beyond the direct use of the body in the care and contact. In addition, there was a great tendency to get into a more concrete way of functioning as opposed to a more symbolic one. I will give a number of examples from different areas that show this concrete functioning as a means of defending against anxiety and mental pain.

MOVING AND IMPROVING

As I have described earlier, the physical moving of patients, in some ways a necessity, was used to create a culture of constant moving that seemed to ignore that being moved might matter to people. I also felt that the moving of patients on the ward was used as a concrete measure to create a sense of improvement.

A patient, Mr F, has apparently deteriorated. He is brought back to the ward and is now put in one of the first two bays, whereas previously he was in a bay further down the corridor. There are not many patients on the ward that day and there are vacant beds in both Bay 1 and Bay 2. I overhear a conversation between Judith and a doctor about the duty shift last night and about something that went wrong. They establish that this was another nurse's fault. When the doctor leaves, Judith says jokingly to him, 'Now there will be no one to accuse me!' A few minutes later Judith speaks to a relative, telling her that the patient will be in a different bay the next day. She explains: 'The further they move down the ward, the better they get.' Then she goes to the board and looks at it for a while. She suggests to Jane that they could move Mr A. Jane has some reservations because Mr A is still on infusions, but then they decide to go ahead with the move. Mr F later seemed to deteriorate even more, because the following week he had been moved again to a single room next to the nurses' desk.

In this observation, a patient's state had deteriorated seriously, and other things had gone wrong too. A feeling of guilt and inadequacy was around. The initial solution was to find someone else to blame (the nurse on the night shift), but Judith's remark ('Now there will be no one to accuse me!') showed that she continued to feel guilty and internally criticised. This sense of guilt and self-doubt was, I think, quite unbearable and had to be counteracted immediately. Then, in her remark to the relative, Judith made a slip of the tongue. Even though the rationale on the ward was that the better patients get the further they are moved down the ward, Judith actually said it the other way round ('The further they move down the ward, the better they get'): behind this slip, I think, lay the wish that concretely moving a patient would in itself reflect improvement. If 'something is moving', there is no need for doubts about one's ability to get patients better or to keep them alive. This concrete rescue from the feelings of guilt and doubt was then instantly put into action: a patient was moved by the nurses, even though there was no actual need to move anyone, and there were even good reasons for *not* moving this particular patient.

REPAIRING INSTEAD OF CURING

The same move, from self-doubts to a concrete form of reassurance, was observable on another day when the physical repairing of an apparatus seemed to be used as a defence against doubts and guilt.

Helen picks up a small item of apparatus, which may have been for blood sugar testing, but she cannot operate it. She turns to Ann who tries as well, again unsuccessfully. Ann sighs and says: 'Everything gets broken in here.' Helen tries to find the manual, but eventually Nancy manages to find the fault in the batteries being low. Once Helen has found new batteries and it works again, she starts speaking to the nurse Peter about a patient who has died. For a moment she seems to feel sad and guilty and says something about the various moves the patient had (presumably wondering whether the death was linked with the moving), but Peter reassures her that the patient was beyond help. 'Once they've reached the stage of . . .' (something I didn't understand), 'one can't really do very much any more.' Then Helen gets up and goes to another nurse and has a pleasant chat with her.

The sentence 'Everything gets broken in here', I think, went beyond the area of broken equipment, but was a reflection of a more general despair about their ability to keep patients alive. One of their patients had died and this had brought up doubts and despair in the nurses. But it seemed difficult to give such thoughts any mental space. Being able to repair a technical device provided them with a reassurance on a very concrete level. Interestingly, after the nurse had been reassured in this way she was able to speak briefly about the death and her doubts and could tolerate feelings of sadness and guilt for a moment, until these feelings were glossed over again quickly.

Self-doubts were also raised through the fact that they were not a real cardiology ward and had to send patients to another hospital for the more sophisticated cardiological investigations like angiography. This constant transfer of patients may have been experienced as a concrete expression of their inadequacy and incompetence. They then tried to compensate by using all sorts of concrete means, such as the ones described or just by filling themselves up with activity.

High activity always seemed to signify value and importance on this ward. On a couple of days a nurse greeted me in the beginning by saying, for example, 'You should have been here an hour ago. We had such an activity!', or 'You are too late, we had chaos here!' One day, only a few weeks after I had started my observations, a nurse was surprised that I was still doing them and wanted to know how long I was going to go on for and how long they were each time. When I said 'for three months' and 'an hour each time', she replied 'Agony!' and then suggested that I make myself a cup of coffee. In this way she conveyed clearly her view that looking, taking in, feeling and thinking about people was like doing nothing, or just 'agony' – so boring that one might as well have a cup of coffee instead. The concrete activity of running around and doing something was seen as valid and important. Even though a lot of activity was needed on this ward, sometimes to an extremely stressful degree, it also became a defensive technique to avoid being burdened by painful feelings and thoughts arising out of real contact with patients.

MAGIC PROTECTION

Concrete protection was used at times against fears of contagion and emotional overburdening, as in the following example.

Near to the nurses' desk, and to where I usually sat, was a single room. In one of my observations nurses started to wear plastic aprons and, at times, gloves when they went into the room, and visitors were asked to put on a plastic apron as well. In one of the following observations,

Jane answers a telephone call. After a while she puts down the receiver and asks Trudy how contagious tuberculosis is. Trudy explains to her about an 'airborne infection' and Jane passes this on to the caller, explaining that TB is an airborne infection and if she wears a plastic apron and gloves it should be OK and no problem. 'Why are you asking?', asks Jane, and continuously tries to reassure the caller who is apparently quite worried. She reiterates a few times that if she wears a plastic apron and gloves it is OK, emphasising that these are the precautions the nurses take themselves. 'What is an airborne infection? It is an infection that you breathe in through the mouth. No, there isn't really any risk, you don't need to worry. Wearing an apron and gloves and washing the hands thoroughly afterwards is sufficient; that's what we do as well.' And after some more talking, 'No, it's highly unlikely that TB symptoms would start within four or five hours.' Eventually Jane finishes the call, laughs, and says contemptuously to Trudy. 'She thinks she has caught TB, and now her symptoms have started.'

I think the fear of contagion was considerable on the ward, not only the fear of contracting a serious infectious disease like tuberculosis but likewise the fear of getting all the other diseases these patients had. But as important was the fear of being infected with all the unwanted feelings patients and relatives brought with them, of anxiety, helplessness, despair and fear of death.

In this vignette, the fear of contagion was dealt with on two levels. First in a concrete way by putting on a plastic apron or gloves. This was in fact not a reasonable protective measure against physical contagion, because a plastic apron could hardly provide any protection against an infection that is 'breathed in through the mouth'. This showed that their anxiety had led to a breakdown of real thinking and to a concrete and unthinking way of functioning. Second, the fears were projected outside and when they returned in the form of a questioning visitor they were ridiculed. In this light, the caller who may have been over-worried appeared like a fool. In this state of mind, no mental space could be allowed for reasonable enquiry or worry. Having rid themselves of reason and worry, the nurses could feel superior, fearless and in control.

RECOVERING FROM THE SHOCK OF DEATH

I would now like to present a detailed vignette which shows some of the defensive techniques I have described in this chapter in operation and illustrates how the serious shock about two sudden deaths was dealt with. The vignette shows both the less and the more defensive ways of functioning: on the one hand a fleeting acknowledgement of sadness and guilt, and on the other frantic excitement, erotisation and a concrete form of regaining control, but also the use of the body for physical play, feeding and affectionate contact.

Coming on the ward I see that a new sign – 'Coronary Care' – has been put up on the windows of the first two bays where monitored patients are kept. When I see the ward sister Nancy, she says to me 'You've come too late!', and adds, 'It's been chaos, we had two arrests!' Then, during the hour, some new patients are announced by telephone. Nancy explains on the phone that they just had two arrests and tries to deflect patients who might also be at risk of dying. Speaking on the phone, she says, 'It's really stressful being a ward sister!', and for a moment appears distressed and burdened. Then she switches to her jolly voice and finishes the call in an almost excited tone, 'Bye, love!'

Another nurse, Helen, speaking on the phone, says sadly: 'He didn't live long, he died, it's a pity!' But then, with a very different voice that seems to leave no room for doubt, 'Oh, yes, I agree, it would have been . . .'

Then Nancy is standing at the board with the bed-numbers and patients' names to update and rearrange. She wipes out names, puts some of them down in a different bay, then wipes some of them out again. Suddenly she sings, 'Oh, I am happy, they're all going home!' Her activity on the board becomes more and more frantic, she changes the patients from one bay to another, backwards and forwards, at great speed.

Two new patients are brought on the ward and attended to. The wife of one of them, an elderly man in a bad state, has to wait on the corridor for a while until Nancy tells her that she can go to her husband now and 'do what you've been wanting to do for a long time, but haven't been able to . . .' The tone and content of this remark appear to have a sexual connotation.

Later, when it is a bit quieter, Nancy stands at the board with others and offers chocolate to them and then to me as well. She and a doctor (who has just certified the death of one of the patients) play with a rubber band, stretching it between them and wondering who will let go of it first. The atmosphere is quite flirtatious between them. Eventually, Nancy and Mary go down the corridor, hand in hand and chatting cheerfully, to have coffee.

My own feelings change during the hour; from a sense of bewilderment (Arrests? Were the police here? Oh, no, these are deaths, how awful!) to a feeling of pity for the nurses, to being absorbed and fascinated by their excited activity, nearly forgetting about the deaths.

This observation shows the aftermath of a real crisis. Two sudden deaths from heart attacks had occurred and the ward was in a massive state of shock. Anxiety was around, as were feelings of disappointment, sadness, guilt and self-doubt. The deaths had occurred just after the nurses had put up the new sign – 'Coronary Care' – as a concrete symbol of pride in their specialised work. So this was quite a blow to their pride and competence and brought their anxieties about death to the fore. The material shows how the ward gradually recovered from the shock and how in this process staff used several of the defensive techniques I have described in this chapter.

There were brief moments in this observation where exhaustion, pity and sadness were expressed. Interestingly, this was done over the telephone more than between each other, as if such feelings were felt to be too dangerous to bring into direct contact between them. Quite appropriately, the ward sister tried to protect herself and the ward from further shocks by making sure she was given new patients who were not at serious risk. The brief expression of exhaustion and sadness was instantly followed by jolliness, excitement and flirtatiousness. Self-doubts were immediately counteracted by reassurance. Anxiety and feelings of sadness, guilt and self-doubt seemed too painful to be allowed more than a moment's space. What took over instead was manic activity, excitement and erotisation. The leaving of patients was turned into a reason for joyful singing. The frantic activity on the board was a concrete way of dealing with the blow and served the aim of regaining a sense of control. Concrete feeding took the place of the emotional feeding that would have been needed, and might have been longed for in this crisis.

These defensive techniques, however, seemed to work in some way, so that the atmosphere that started off very tense and anxious relaxed and was cheerful and playful again at the end. However, no working through of the deaths had taken place and the deeply defensive culture had been re-established.

DISCUSSION

I have tried to give an account of my observations of the life and functioning of a general medical ward which I observed regularly during a period of four months. I have tried to understand my observations from a psychoanalytic perspective, looking at the anxieties and painful feelings stirred up in the staff by their work and at the defences they used, individually and collectively, to deal with these anxieties and feelings.

Working with suffering, physically ill and sometimes dying patients stirs up painful feelings of various kinds: pity and sadness, resentment and guilt, fear of illness, contagion and death, doubts about one's ability to care for the patients and to keep them alive, and helplessness. The direct and intimate contact with bodies also arouses sexual impulses and the anxieties connected with them. On this particular ward, with the frequent discharge and transfer of patients, feelings around loss, of sadness, anger and guilt, were also important.

A particular culture developed on the ward, built up of a set of defensive techniques. The general atmosphere of the ward was characterised by friendliness and jolliness, but the friendly contact was usually fleeting and superficial, thus avoiding contact of any depth which could stir up more troublesome feelings. Any painful experience of loss was usually prevented by the general tendency to form quick and superficial attachments from which they could detach themselves again equally quickly.

The frequent transfers and discharges of patients made it more necessary to find ways of dealing with loss. However, this was done by creating a defensive culture of constant moving in which the significance of loss was largely denied. Patients were frequently moved, much more than necessary, as if they were movable objects rather than human beings who minded losing their personal links and their own place. Thus relationships were broken up, not by moving nurses, as Menzies ([1959] 1988) described, but by moving the patients themselves. Staff often turned quite actively away from the human suffering, by physically looking away or by turning to jolliness and excitement, thereby freeing themselves from an experience of demand on them and of guilt.

Jolliness, excitement and a flirtatious, erotic atmosphere were characteristic of this ward on which there often seemed to be no space for proper thinking. Excitement and sexualisation are powerful defences against depression and fear of death, and some of the observations have illustrated how in the face of depression and death the ward staff became excited and flirtatious with each other. The quick recoveries and the successes one can experience with some of the heart patients could potentially foster a sense of omnipotence and may have contributed to this manic tendency. In this superficial, jolly atmosphere staff seemed to infantilise the patients, and the jolliness also contained an element of compliance where neither nurses nor patients appeared able to complain about the pressures put on them, or the way they were treated.

While much of the work on a medical ward necessarily centres on the bodies rather than the minds of the patients, this ward became a 'world of bodies' where the body took on enormous importance, to a degree that people often were not sufficiently related to as whole persons. The body was used as a means of communication and defence. Physical contact, like touching and embracing, was common amongst nurses, and in their contact with patients, as concrete expressions of care and affection. This bodily and concrete world extended further, to concrete forms of defence which were used to a large extent. The moving of patients on the ward, for example, was used far beyond what seemed necessary to create a constant movement, ignoring the emotional impact on the people; in addition it became a concrete substitute for improving.

This concrete functioning and the extensive use of the body were quite different from what has been observed on psychiatric wards. The fact that it is primarily the patients' bodies, rather than their minds, that are ill and the focus of care, may be an important reason for this difference. In this form of care the body lends itself more easily for a defensive use. Very different from psychiatric wards was also the atmosphere of excitement and eroticism. This contrasted strongly with the flattening of affects and deadening of human encounters, which Chiesa (Chapter 5) and Donati (Chapter 3) observed on psychiatric wards. This deadening was explained by Donati as deriving from the fear that any liveliness could lead to madness and violence. On this cardiological ward, however, the anxiety was much more about death. Liveliness and manic excitement were therefore felt as a reassurance against the fear of death.

The system of defences was not completely rigid. I have illustrated that the nurses showed the ability to experience painful feelings and think about them. They expressed concern, sadness, guilt and their sense of burden. However, this mental space was usually closed off quickly under the pressure of stress, anxiety and mental pain and then a deeply defensive culture emerged. I have shown that the atmosphere could at times be more open but that this openness was quickly closed off and the anxieties that human contact with suffering people brought with it were warded off. Such dynamics in groups where a 'reflective space' is closed off, because powerful feelings lead to attacks on this space, have been described by Hinshelwood (1994).

On this ward, the reason for the closing-off lay, I think, in more than just the nature of the work with physically ill patients and the anxieties it stirred up. The nurses were carrying additional heavy burdens, many of which came from the pressures of the internal market which the lead nurse hinted at in the initial meeting: financial pressures, bed shortages, performance checks from the purchaser and the insecurity of their jobs. And there were further pressures from the way the hospital was organised: doctors were not attached to specific wards and the nurses were very much on their own. As Chiesa (Chapter 5) points out, such external influences may have a strong bearing on the work, and knowledge about them may add an important dimension to what is directly observable. On the ward that I observed, the nurses didn't seem to have sufficient help and containment in dealing with the enormous burden from either the work with the patients or from such external pressures.

The joke of one of the nurses in the initial staff meeting that I could sit at the desk and answer the telephone took on a different meaning during the course of my observations. The telephone represented the boundary between the ward and the outside, and this aspect was disturbing for them, as they could never know what would come next through the telephone. I think they wished for a more protective boundary which could provide some containment, and this wish was immediately directed towards the observer. The pressures of the new NHS system represent a breakdown of proper boundaries. Inhuman, pure financial pressures intrude into the world of human suffering and care. This causes further deep anxieties beyond the ones that the nursing work inevitably brings with it, and this must have increased the need for a defensive culture on this ward.

Chapter 9

Nowhere to hide

A day case centre

Debbie Maxwell

INTRODUCTION

This study took place in the Day Case Centre of a university teaching hospital in weekly visits over a period of three months. The centre, set up a few years ago, operates as an independent unit within the hospital and is designed to facilitate the smooth and efficient transition of day case surgical patients through the various stages of the treatment process from pre-assessment, prior to admission into hospital, through to post-operative care after the patient has returned home.

In a hospital day case centre, the nurses and clinical personnel are not faced with physically ill or injured patients, indeed the patients present mainly as physically healthy people, and the treatments could be regarded in some cases as being purely cosmetic. However, even though the conditions being dealt with are not life threatening, outcomes are still uncertain and there is always a potential risk to the patient both from the anaesthetic and the operation itself. Those in the helping professions inevitably and repeatedly encounter failure in their work, and within the NHS, ever-increasing pressure on time and resources, together with the emphasis on cost-effectiveness, reduction of waiting lists, performance checks and audit, leads to additional difficulties and anxieties. Along with these organisational demands, and the medical task itself, clinical personnel also have to deal with the anxieties and conflicts implicit in the relationship with the anxious patient.

For nurses and clinical personnel working in a day case centre, the brief but intense relationships with the patients may generate anxieties and conflicting feelings; there may be resentment and envy for the treatment provided, as well as fear and guilt for the damage that may be caused by their intrusion into generally well functioning bodies. In a situation where there is often intimate contact, but no real opportunity for nurses and patients to get to know one another, there may also be a fear of the sexual impulses raised. In this particular day case centre the constant intrusions may have led to feelings of resentment, and the physical and emotional exposure may have generated a need to escape from the embarrassment, awkwardness and emotional distress.

The clinical personnel often showed an ability to be sensitive, and to think about the feelings aroused; however, a defensive culture developed whereby the organisational process seemed to take over and replace relations between people. Certain thoughts, feelings and experiences, felt as too difficult to experience and think about, were pushed out of conscious awareness, both individually and collectively, by the use of various defensive techniques.

The study investigates the culture of the day case centre, and looks at the techniques used to defend against the anxieties and mental pain generated by the short but intense and intimate relationships with the patients. Amongst the defensive techniques observed were embarrassing intrusiveness, a depersonalisation and denial of the individual, retreat behind boundaries, and defensive use of space as a means of protecting one's personal privacy and shutting out the anxiety.

THE HOSPITAL AND THE CENTRE

The space

The day case centre was comprised of various physically defined spaces, each fulfilling a particular function in the treatment process. Unlike a ward situation where patients leave for operations, returning later, in the day case centre the patients entered at one point and moved through from one area and process to another, rather like objects on a production line.

On a preliminary visit to the day case centre to meet the consultant anaesthetist, I was taken aback when I entered the reception area to the sight and sound of a piano being played. With a TV on, carpeted floors, co-ordinated colours and finishes, soft furnishings and an abundance of plants, the general ambience was more like a hotel reception than that of a general NHS hospital. I was shown through into the operational part of the centre, where the co-ordinated finishes continued from reception through double doors, up a corridor past lockers on the right, a toilet and changing room on the left, into the patient assessment and observation space. Individual upholstered armchairs were positioned around the edges and there was a TV and hi-fi unit in one corner. In the centre were two tables with small baskets of pot pourri and boxes of tissues, and other tables around the edge with magazines on. Upholstered stools were stored under and beside some of the chairs. There was no direct natural light, except that from a window, through which I could see what appeared to be a painted view of trees, hills, and water. Two assessment rooms opened directly into the area, and double doors led out of the area through to the operating theatres.

Opposite the seating area was a nursing station, positioned centrally between the assessment and recovery spaces, with a reception counter and access through to recovery and the departure lounge. Around the walls of assessment space were a few small pictures and a pin board. On the walls to either side of the nursing station were perspex boards on which were handwritten the names of the surgeon and nurse assigned to each operating list for that day. The operating lists, on typed A4 sheets, were taped to the perspex boards, although patient names and operations were only visible at close inspection.

The process

The observation took place over a three-month period on a weekly basis for one hour at the same time each week, during the early phase of a morning session – between 8.00 and 9.00 a.m. Three operating lists were scheduled for this day of the week: ophthalmic, dental and vascular (varicose vein), although sometimes there were only two lists running. During the observation hour, patients were collected individually from the reception area by a nurse and shown through to the observation space and into a changing room to change into hospital gown, dressing gown and socks. The patient's belongings were stored in a locker for safe-keeping and the patient then waited in the observation space to be assessed by the nurse, anaesthetist and surgeon. After being assessed, the patient waited again to be called for the operation (which may have been a period of up to two hours), when s/he was shown through to theatre by an assigned nurse.

The people

Within the day case centre there was a team of female nursing staff, comprised of registered nurses and auxiliary workers, caring for the patients during the pre-operative and post-operative stages of the treatment process. Each operating list had an assigned nurse, who was responsible for caring for each patient on her list, although some of the tasks were carried out by an auxiliary nurse. Other clinical personnel, both male and female, who took part in the assessment processes were anaesthetists, consultant surgeons and/or their registrars and medical students. Whereas the assigned nurse was a constant figure during the hour, the anaesthetists, surgeons and medical students would make only a brief appearance. I was introduced informally to some of the nursing staff; there was, however, no introduction to any of the other clinical personnel. During the course of the observations there was only one nurse who was there every week; the other nurses and clinical personnel varied from week to week, some appearing more regularly than others. All nurses and clinical personnel, regardless of experience, discipline, function or gender wore theatre greens.

During the observation hour there would usually be between three and eight patients in the assessment space, male and female, with ages ranging from teenagers to the elderly. Patients were identifiable by their hospital gown, dressing gown and socks, and were usually unaccompanied, although relatives were allowed to wait with them until they were taken through to theatre. I was not introduced to any of the patients.

Initial thoughts

My initial discussion with the consultant anaesthetist gave me the impression that the staff were proud of the centre as a whole. I was told that it was regarded as a model for day case centres in the country, and that the efficiency of day case treatments had improved enormously since the new centre had been opened, with cancellations and non-attendances being reduced substantially. However, she was interested in any suggestions for improvement as the staff generally felt that this particular space did not work as well as they would like, although they weren't sure why. Comments were made about the low lighting levels and depressing colours, but concern was also expressed about the hospital gowns, which being one-size only meant that patients were often bodily and sexually exposed. For this reason patients were allowed to bring their own dressing gowns. The consultant showed me around the different areas, explaining their functions and introduced me informally to some of the nurses at the tea station.

My visit to the centre was in-between morning and afternoon sessions, and although empty of patients the space in which I was to observe felt very cramped. Recalling my own experiences as a hospital patient, and specifically as an ophthalmic day case patient in a London general hospital, I felt very uncomfortable at the thought of being so exposed and in full view of everyone, and with apparently no privacy.

As an observer, my role was to observe events and interactions, note the feelings and states evoked for me during the observation and then try to verify the place of these within the observation experience. My aim was to be as unobtrusive as possible, keeping my interactions with staff and patients to a minimum. (The method is described in more detail in Chapter 2.) However, anxieties were raised in my mind about how I would be able to remain unobtrusive and manage my boundaries in such an exposed space; also, how I would cope with the discomfort of being without the protection of a socially understood role such as that of friend or relative. These anxieties seemed to be reflected in my dilemma of what to wear. Should I wear a hospital gown and be the same as the patients so as not to look conspicuous, risking the embarrassment of being mistaken for a patient or the hostility of staff and patients at being an impostor, or should I wear my own casual clothes and stand out as being different and feeling more like an intruder? After much consideration I decided to wear my own clothes, feeling somehow safer in the belief that I would not feel so exposed, retain my own identity and be able to justify my position if challenged. This dilemma seemed to reflect my concern about how to manage the anxieties associated with my intrusion, albeit for a short time only, into this organisational body.

THE OBSERVATION

Embarrassing intrusiveness

The general atmosphere within the centre was comfortable and very friendly, and I observed how the patients would often be addressed in a light-hearted, jokey manner. However, there was sometimes a rather embarrassing intrusiveness in the way that the patients were treated. Changing and assessment processes would often be interrupted by a nurse in an exposing way, as the assessment/changing rooms opened directly into the observation space. I was often able to see and hear what was going on through open doors and thin walls, leaving me feeling embarrassed and intrusive. Whilst the nurses often seemed sensitive to the nature and difficulties inherent in physical and sexual exposure in front of a stranger, or discussion of intimate bodily functions, at other times they seemed unaware of their embarrassing intrusiveness into the patient's physical and emotional space.

Early in observation 11,

a middle-aged female patient is brought through by the assigned nurse, and shown into assessment room 2 to change. I hear the nurse, Sarah, ask the patient whether she has got a dressing gown and then say that she'll go and fetch one. A short while later, with dressing gown in hand, she returns to room 2, knocks on the door and opening it slightly asks 'Are you decent?' Pausing, she then opens the door and goes in. 'That was good timing', she says, and closes the door behind her.

Later on in the same observation,

I hear a patient being shown into one of the changing rooms out of my view, and the nurse Jane saying loudly: 'Right, everything off', and then 'Stick your head out when you're ready.' I assume the patient to be a man by the nurse's manner of speech and feel rather embarrassed. The nurse returns shortly afterwards and I hear her say to the patient something about 'Yes they are difficult aren't they', and then 'Cover up your decency, we don't want you flashing' – again loudly enough for me to hear clearly.

In the first example, Sarah showed some sensitivity for the patient's need for privacy whilst undressing, and there also seemed to be a recognition of both her own and the patient's potential discomfort and embarrassment around the intimate nature of getting undressed and exposing oneself both physically and sexually to a stranger. In the second example, Jane seemed to deal with her difficult and conflicting emotions by making light of the situation rather loudly, possibly to make the feelings less frightening. However, she also seemed to deny the patient's adult male sexuality by first addressing him in a rather infantilising manner, and subsequently by asking him to cover his genitals so as not to expose his sexuality.

In a day case centre very intimate procedures are being performed when there is no opportunity for real intimacy to develop, and for both patients and nurses the intimacy of dealing with physical and sexual exposure, as well as bodily functions, with a stranger may lead to some difficult and conflicting emotions. On several occasions during the undressing and assessment processes I saw patients in a state of undress, such as in my ninth observation:

One of the nurses knocks on room 1 and opens the door. I can see a female patient standing in the room exposed up to her groin. I feel horrified at this level of exposure and very uncomfortable, wanting them to close the door. The door is closed, but a short time afterwards is opened again, exposing the patient once more.

I felt embarrassed but also both intrusive and intruded upon, and longed to escape from the exposure and vulnerability with which I was confronted. This may well have reflected some of the patient's undoubted feelings of being physically and emotionally exposed and intruded upon. However, for the nursing staff, who were constantly confronted with physical and sexual exposure, there may have been an intense longing to escape from the difficult feelings that were aroused by such brief but intimate contact with a stranger, reflected in a denial of the importance of personal privacy and leading to the sometimes embarrassing intrusiveness observed.

Fear of damage

My main anxiety was associated with the impact that my intrusive explorations into the internal workings and dynamics of part of this ostensibly healthy and well-functioning organisational body may have.

Working in the day case centre and having to perform intimate and intrusive procedures on parts of individuals who are, as a whole, in good physical working order may raise anxieties about causing damage, generating feelings of concern and guilt. And of course, sometimes this can be a reality – patients do get upset and operations can go wrong, resulting in damage. I observed the emphasis placed on following the checklists and procedures, perhaps as a means of defending against the anxieties raised, and the fear of getting it wrong. The nurses may have also felt resentment and envy for the treatment being provided for such minor cases, fearing their own hostility towards the patients. The following vignette from observation 13 shows how one nurse battled with her conflicting feelings whilst attending to two female ophthalmic patients.

Jane is talking to patient 'A', whilst putting drops in her left eye, and explaining that it may sting a little. A while later she returns to give her some more eye drops, after which the patient seems to be in some discomfort and tries to rub her eye. Jane advises her not to 'if she possibly can' as she may rub the drops away . . . Later on, Jane is explaining to another ophthalmic patient 'B' about the drops that she's going to have to put in her eyes and that they may sting – but that she doesn't do it maliciously. She then shouts loudly over to an elderly male patient (who she had apparently attended on a previous occasion) in a joking fashion 'I don't do it maliciously, do I, Henry?' He doesn't seem to understand that this is directed at him and doesn't respond. I feel quite uncomfortable and embarrassed by having to witness this interaction, and Jane then says to him, 'You're supposed to say no', at which point the female patient says under her breath, but loudly enough for me to hear, 'Even if you mean yes.'

Jane seemed to be desperately trying to escape from her feelings of anxiety and guilt, unsuccessfully seeking some reassurance that her intrusion was not malicious. However, the patient seemed to be feeling the underlying hostility, possibly reflected by my own discomfort with the interaction.

Depersonalisation and denial of the individual

I observed how each person was stripped of any individual distinctiveness, and categorised – becoming either a patient or a member of the clinical personnel, identifiable, respectively, by hospital gowns, dressing gowns and socks, or by theatre greens. Contact between individuals was often fleeting, and although there were times when I wished I was invisible, there were also times I longed for some acknowledgement as an individual; however, passing comments such as 'Good morning, sorry, I didn't see you there'; 'Oh, are you early?', and 'You're in the wrong chair' would leave me feeling isolated, intrusive and unwanted.

In my first observation,

a man in theatre greens approaches and crouches between myself and an elderly female patient. He explains to her that the consultant surgeon himself will not be able to perform the operation due to unforeseen circumstances;

however, as senior registrar he will be happy to do the operation if she is in agreement. I feel myself immediately react, recalling my own emotions when being confronted with a similar situation as a patient. I feel shocked, angry, upset and let down that the relationship with the consultant has not been maintained. However, the patient, who seems to have difficulty in remembering the surgeon's name, eventually nods, saying that she doesn't want to go away again and that 'You're all the same anyway.'

With relationships being so transient in the day case centre, the patient may have had hardly any contact with the consultant, and indeed she found it hard to remember his name, perhaps picking up on the fleeting contact and the atmosphere of 'no relationship' where everyone was the same. This also seemed to be reflected in the exposed nature of the interaction, which perhaps afforded some protection for the surgeon against the anxieties raised by direct contact with the individual.

In contrast to my own experience of being a day case patient and of having clear physical boundaries – my own space and privacy in the form of a bed, locker and curtain – there seemed to be a blurring of physical, personal and psychological boundaries. Although I observed that often there would be a direct interaction between nurse and patient during the assessment processes, sometimes there would simply be a move in and out of the patient's space without any real contact being made, almost as if no one would notice and there would be no effect.

In observation 4,

a male patient arrives and takes a seat opposite me. Soon afterwards he is shown into a changing room by one of the nurses, who apologises for it being rather small, but explains that there is no other available space. A few minutes later a female patient comes out of an assessment room and sits in the chair where the male patient had been sitting. When he emerges from the changing room in his hospital gown and dressing gown, he walks around the corner to return to his seat, but his chair is now occupied. He hesitates, moves to another chair, sits down putting his bag down beside the chair and starts to read his newspaper. A few minutes later another nurse walks over to where he is sitting, picks up his bag without saying a word and takes it away, locking it in one of the lockers. From where he is sitting, the patient cannot see where she is taking it. He looks around and seems unsure about what is happening; however, he remains seated and does not say anything, returning his attention to his paper. I want to help, to explain what has happened, but I feel helpless and unable to do or say anything – stripped.

Individual identities and boundaries were lost, with patients and staff alike moving in and out of one another's spaces as if there was no impact. If I could not sit in 'my place', because of someone else's intrusion (as happened twice), I would feel upset, estranged and displaced, perhaps reflecting feelings that the patients may very well have shared. My desire to hold onto 'my place' also seemed to be reflected in my decision to wear my own clothes, enabling me in some way to hold onto my role, individual identity and personal privacy. For the clinical personnel also, the need to hang onto some individuality, identity and personal privacy may have been particularly important in a culture where these were stripped away. I observed how one nurse turned up her trouser legs, perhaps as a way of retaining some individuality and identity.

In observation 5,

the vascular surgeon enters the assessment area, and walks quickly over to the operating list, apologising meekly to sister Karen for being late. He asks about a patient and is directed through to the rooms in the recovery area. As he walks through, he comments in an irritated way that he couldn't find his trousers, and had to take someone else's which had been used and were smelly. A few minutes later nurse Trisha runs quickly over to assessment room 1 and asks nurse Jane to vacate the room. Jane says that she is just finishing with the patient, and Trisha hurries her. The surgeon comes marching back into the area shouting that the clinic starts at 8.30 a.m. and it's late. He storms through the doors leading to the operating theatres, slamming the doors against the wall. The nurses are running around frantically justifying their actions to one another. Trisha is explaining to Karen that she had tried to vacate a room and that it was only one minute past 8.30. I feel very uncomfortable, and wonder what the patients make of all this. The surgeon returns, followed by various nurses and students, and walks over to the operating list. Jane says good morning to him and he snaps back that it is not a good morning, and he could not find his trousers. Jane says she is just trying to be friendly. I want to disappear through a little hole in the floor, and try to avoid his gaze, but eventually I catch his eye and he calls out across the area that he hopes I'm making a note of all of this. I nod my head, wishing I was not there at this moment. He then calls a patient into an assessment room. The atmosphere is tense – the nurses are all still rushing around. Karen is talking to a lady in a suit at the end of the corridor. When the surgeon emerges from the assessment room, he sternly tells the nurses to get the patient ready for surgery, and marches through the doors to the operating theatres. Suddenly I am aware that there are no nurses – they have all disappeared.

Perhaps, for the surgeon, the loss of 'his' trousers symbolised an intrusion into his personal space and privacy as well as a loss of identity, leaving him exposed and vulnerable with nothing to hold on to. His own fear, confusion and panic, expressed as anger and frustration at the clinic being 'late' were forcefully projected onto the nurses who then ran around in a state of panic desperately trying to justify their actions and feeling the displaced guilt of being late. The panic followed by the physical disappearance of the nurses reflected my own difficulty in dealing with the emotional outburst, and my wish to disappear from the scene.

Several minutes later, sister Karen reappears from the direction of the office and approaches a female vascular patient, 'A', who is waiting in the corridor, saying that it looks as if the toilet is engaged. She offers to show the patient to another toilet, and then asks if 'A' has been shown where she goes after the operation. 'A' says that she hasn't been and Karen asks her if she'd like to see. The patient says yes and they both move through to the recovery area. When Karen returns with 'A', she sits down on the table between us. We smile at one another in a friendly way and 'A' picks up a magazine from the table, commenting on one of the headlines "WHEN SURGERY KILLS". We all laugh, but after the recent outburst I wonder about the patient's underlying anxiety about the operation she is about to have. Karen explains that the surgeon did apologise, 'sort of', and goes on to explain that there are set procedures to follow, but if something upsets the system, like a patient who can't be processed, then the whole schedule is upset. She explains how this morning all the bedrooms on the other side were occupied by children, so there was no overflow space available for the surgeon to do his assessment at that time. 'A' enquires about how long she will be waiting, and Karen says about an hour. She then says she'll check, and walks over to the board. She confirms that it will be about an hour, and 'A' says she'll read then – but maybe not the article about 'When Surgery Kills'.

In the above vignette there was quite a different atmosphere, with Karen showing genuine interest and concern for the patient's well-being – direct contact between individuals rather than the fleeting, passing contact which I often observed. The surgeon's intrusion – the swift but rather violent in-and-out of physical and psychological space – seemed to reflect the nature of the work in the day case centre. The impact of the violent intrusion could not be denied, the underlying anxiety of the patient being communicated with the magazine headline. For the nurses, however, perhaps finding some physical space and personal privacy away from the intensity of the experience also provided sufficient space to think about the experience and the potential damage caused to the psychological well-being of the patients, allowing a shift from the detached and distant patient–nurse relationship to one of direct and close contact between individual personalities.

As an observer, I was conspicuous by my difference and very aware of my intrusion as a stranger, which aroused various reactions: curiosity, suspicion, and expectations, including a request for me to present my findings formally. I experienced a constant conflict between wanting to be acknowledged as an individual and wanting to hide in the patient group, reflected in my early dilemma about what to wear.

I sometimes longed for contact; however, over a period of weeks I received some rather unexpected but very direct attention from the nursing staff: the sister suggested that I could wear a hospital gown and dressing gown like the patients, so that I 'wouldn't look so conspicuous'; and remarks from nurses such as 'Are you sure you don't want to be a patient?', 'I told you we should put her in a theatre gown' and 'Get that lady in a theatre gown!' My initial response to these remarks was to laugh, but I began to feel increasingly uncomfortable, experiencing this as an intrusion into my private space and threatening my personal identity.

In observation 8,

I arrive to find that my usual place is occupied by a patient. Feeling somewhat destabilised and panicky, I return to my original position where I note my feeling of exposure . . . Soon afterwards the sister walks by, looks at me and says 'It might be a bit dangerous sitting there.' I wonder what on earth she means, and feel quite threatened and nervous after she says this. Later on, one of the auxiliary nurses is attending to an elderly female patient, explaining that she may have to have her nail varnish removed. The nurse is also carrying a roll of tape and has just taped another patient's earring to her ear. She then turns, walks over to me and asks if I've got nail varnish on, and then whether I want my rings taped. I laugh briefly, but then feel very threatened as she approaches me with her roll of tape, finding myself physically trying to back out of the chair, and saying 'You're not taping anything!' . . . I feel as if I'm losing control, and find myself questioning my own identity – who am I?, am I or am I not a patient? The nurse laughs and, turning away, says 'Oh but you're a relative aren't you' – despite the fact that she has seen me on many occasions before. This feels like a dangerous place to be! I feel anxious and uncomfortable, wanting to get up and leave.

In the face of this intrusion into my personality I experienced feelings of fear, confusion and panic – fear of losing my identity, confusion as to who I was and panic of losing control, perhaps reflecting feelings that the surgeon may have had. I experienced an intense desire to leave the situation, finding the feelings very hard to stay with. However, as an observer, I was intruding into a cultural process that had no place for individuality or the category of observer. It seemed as if the culture could not adapt and find a place for the personal individuality which I represented, and as such set about trying to change me. If I were to become a patient or even a relative, the nurses would no longer have to deal with the anxiety raised by my intrusive presence in their organisational body, and the uncertainty of the outcome.

RETREAT BEHIND A BOUNDARY

In any profession which works with people there is a psychological need for the members to develop a certain degree of professional detachment. However, it seemed that in such an exposed space, with constant intrusions but without any physical boundaries or personal privacy, there was a need to escape from the intensity of the experience – to put up psychological boundaries in order to create some distance and to provide some protection from the anxiety.

Even though patients in the day case centre pass through quickly, the relationships are intense, at times involving intimate physical contact. As well as having to deal with different patients, who are there for the day only, the nursing team also have to deal with the intrusion of different clinical personnel and medical students, who may also just be attending the centre on that particular day. Whereas the assigned nurse was a constant figure during the hour, the anaesthetists, surgeons and medical students would make only a brief appearance, although they often made quite an impact in terms of numbers and level of activity. However, they moved in and out of the spaces quickly, often without appearing to make any real contact with anyone, in the same way that they moved in and out of my mental space, disappearing from my mind once they had physically left the area. I became aware later on in the observations that I had not made any note of one male member of staff who each week would enter and leave the area within the space of a few minutes. Sometimes I would find myself forgetting about patients, as the nurses also seemed to, once they had moved out of one space and into another. In observation 5 I became aware that I could not remember a patient who had been in one of the assessment rooms for rather a long time. One of the nurses suddenly remembered and opened the door, saying 'The doctor should have completed the sentence and told you to come out.' In observation 10 a patient had remained in an assessment room after an examination by the vascular surgeon, and was eventually remembered by a nurse who, on finding the patient, says 'Oh you poor thing – have you been in here all this while.' Similarly, once a patient had been taken through to theatre it was as if they had never been there.

In a situation where every relationship is brief and transient but intense, the nurses and clinical personnel may experience difficulties in balancing the need to remain emotionally detached as a means of protection, with the need to make friendly contact not only with the patients but also with other clinical personnel. It may also be hard for the nursing staff to develop the feeling of a whole staff team, possibly leading to feelings of resentment and difficulties of knowing who is who and in managing or negotiating various personal peculiarities.

In observation 6,

a man in theatre greens, unfamiliar to me, walks through into the area carrying a briefcase. He looks around, and Jane, who is attending to a patient, smiles and says 'Hello' in a very friendly manner, asking him if he would like a coffee. He says 'No thanks', and Jane says loudly that she had no intention of making him one, just of pointing him in the right direction. I flinch . . . and he looks rather embarrassed, retreating behind the desk at the nursing station.

Yet another intrusion seems too much and the balance cannot be maintained. Jane retreats behind a defensive psychological barrier, assuming a demand on her, whilst the man withdraws and retreats to the safety of the nursing station.

I observed how forms and procedures were also used to maximise the distance – emotionally and psychologically – between the patients and the clinical personnel such as in the following vignette from observation 5:

The dental surgeon is talking with her nurse assistant standing at the operating list with their backs to the patients. They are discussing whether a patient is there. His notes are apparently there and they are looking at the dental x-ray. However, the nurse seems convinced that the patient is not, looking at the list at the nursing station and pointing. The surgeon explains that if his notes are there then the patient must be. The patient, whose actual name is then mentioned, calls out in response, and the nurse and surgeon both turn and acknowledge him. The surgeon reiterates to the nurse how the notes wouldn't be there if the patient wasn't.

The clinical personnel also seemed to use the physical space to distance themselves from the patients, and at times there almost seemed to be an invisible boundary between the passive patient waiting area and the active nursing station. Indeed, I observed what seemed to be a passive submission on the part of the patients to whatever was presented by the clinical personnel, as illustrated in earlier vignettes. This passivity was reflected in the general lack of movement by the patients, and in a corresponding lack of verbal communication with the clinical personnel: once, in a situation when a nurse asked patients if anyone would like the TV or radio on, no one responded in any way; as a result the nurse eventually walked off.

As patients, we may want to feel helpless and inadequate (Conran 1985) and dependent on clinical staff to think and make decisions for us. In a day case centre patients may also feel very guilty for taking up valuable time, space and resources with their minor needs. For the day case centre nursing team, who are not subject to the shift working familiar to many nursing practices, there may be feelings of guilt that they are not pulling their weight. I had been informed that some of the staff had been found work in the day case centre after the closure of another local hospital, perhaps also leading to feelings that they are undeserving, dependent and inadequate. The sister, in fact, on several occasions took time out to explain to me how it may look sometimes as if they are not very busy, as if feeling the need to justify their roles and worthiness to me. These feelings of dependency and neediness may then be projected into the patients who, in turn, may identify with them, projecting their capacity for thought and critical judgement into the clinical personnel. Being looked after in luxury surroundings with individual and personal attention may also arouse feelings of guilt and unworthiness in the patients, making it difficult for them to make personal and emotional demands on the staff.

As an observer I also felt the need to remain emotionally detached and unobtrusive. However, I became aware that I would sometimes try to enter and leave the observation space unnoticed, without making direct contact with anyone. Indeed upon entering my penultimate observation the sister said, 'I see they let you sneak through on your own this week.' Although at times I longed for some personal contact and recognition as an individual, at other times I found myself wanting to escape from any direct attention to myself. I felt very protective of my physical, emotional and psychological space and if a patient came and sat next to me or tried to make contact with me I would often feel very uncomfortable and intruded upon, wanting to get away both physically and psychologically.

In observation 10,

a male vascular patient, who I had seen physically exposed in an assessment room a few minutes earlier, comes and sits next to me. I feel immediately that my space has been intruded upon and am uncomfortable at the close proximity, and his male sexuality. The patient is involved in sorting through his briefcase, and doesn't seem to be interested in making contact, much to my relief. However, feeling tense, I find myself just looking ahead and trying to ignore his presence.

In observation 12,

there is a conversation about wisdom teeth going on between two female patients. I feel I am being drawn into the interaction as the elderly patient keeps looking at me and smiling. I look at the clock – it is 8.55 – I feel uncomfortable – I want to get up and go before my time is up. I smile back occasionally but find it very uncomfortable and keep looking away. A part of me wants very much to join in, but the other part wants to get up and leave. I am relieved when it is time for me to go. I put on my jacket and leave. As I walk down the corridor just past the nursing station, I hear a 'bye' from the sister. I stop in my tracks and a 'bye' comes awkwardly out of my mouth. I don't even look around. I feel guilty.

Perhaps my desire to move in and out without being noticed – to deny the impact of my intrusion – reflects both the nature of a day case centre itself, where contact is brief but intense, and the attempts of the staff to deny the impact of their physical and psychological intrusion upon one another and the patients.

Safety in numbers

In the day case centre I observed how the majority of assessments would be carried out by the assigned nurse, anaesthetist and surgeon in the waiting area itself, in full view of, and often within hearing range of, other patients, relatives, staff and myself. Although the two assessment rooms were usually in constant use, the clinical personnel often did not check to see if a room was available or try to find a private space, such as in observation 8:

A female patient – sitting close to me in one of the centrally positioned chairs – is being looked after by a nurse, Jane, who is attending the vascular list. Jane has taken her blood pressure and temperature, when a lady in theatre greens – who is unfamiliar to me – introduces herself to the patient as the anaesthetist and sits down next to her. Jane is standing nearby and the anaesthetist asks her if there is a room free. Jane hesitates and looks over to the assessment rooms, then says that they could use a bedroom. The anaesthetist seems to be waiting for more guidance or directions, but none is forthcoming from Jane and the anaesthetist doesn't ask. She returns her attention to the patient and begins to ask her questions. As far as I am aware, both assessment rooms are free.

Although the anaesthetist initially asked about a private space, she did not pursue the matter with the nurse, who seemed rather unhelpful. Indeed, I observed that generally there was no open acknowledgement by the nurses or clinical personnel of a patient's need for privacy, the likely anxiety or possible embarrassment and discomfort at being looked at and heard by a group of total strangers. Although there were many comments made by the clinical personnel about the lack of space, it seemed almost as if the exposed setting was somehow preferable, safer, the group perhaps affording some protection against the anxiety generated by the intensity of direct contact between individual personalities in a private setting. However, the patients neither questioned the exposure nor demanded privacy. Recalling my own experiences as a hospital patient, I would find it far easier to contain or perhaps even deny my anxiety in an open situation with others around, or one where students were included in the examination or assessment. It would be in situations of privacy, with one to one direct contact with the clinician, where the anxiety and emotion would often be hard to conceal. So perhaps the lack of private space in some ways suited both patients and clinical personnel. Interestingly, I observed that all the surgical vascular assessments were undertaken in privacy, with space often having to be sought in the recovery area. However, the surgeon who usually undertook the operating list on this particular day was often attended by a group of two or more medical students, perhaps again providing some level of protection from this intensity.

For those working in the day case centre, the level of exposure, the lack of privacy and the continual raw confrontation with embarrassing and anxiety-provoking experiences may well have generated a need to escape, but there was nowhere to go. Perhaps hiding one's individual personality in such an exposed setting, withdrawing and becoming indistinguishable from others within the group, disappearing into the mass – may then afford some protection against the intrusiveness of an environment that allows no personal privacy.

Shutting out the anxiety

I observed few open expressions of anxiety from the patients in the day case centre, and indeed I was informed that very anxious patients were usually taken to the private bedrooms in the recovery area, where children were also seen. The atmosphere was usually jolly, and whilst the nursing staff were sometimes sensitive to the patients' concerns, any anxiety expressed was often dealt with in rather a jokey, sometimes sexualised way, and moved away from quickly, both mentally and physically such as in a vignette from observation 6:

A young female ophthalmic patient looks a bit concerned as Jane talks about putting the thermometer in her ear, saying that it won't hurt. After taking her blood pressure, they are talking and I hear the patient say 'terrified' in a jokey sort of way. Jane goes on to explain about measuring her legs for the 'sexy' stockings, then goes off.

Jane is unable to stay with the patient's anxiety, the sexualisation perhaps acting as a defence against the fear of damage. In the following vignette from observation 3, a male ophthalmic patient of non-British origins was being assessed by the assigned nurse, with his son acting as an interpreter.

Talking in a loud voice to the son, nurse Anne explains that after the operation his father will not be able to see out of the eye – only a bright light – but the eye will be covered. The son communicates this to his father. She goes on to say that a nurse will be holding his hand all the way through the operation, and that if at any time he is in any discomfort he is to squeeze the nurse's hand and they will stop. I presume from this that he will only be under a local anaesthetic. I think about how terrifying it must be to not be able to communicate, or to make oneself understood and to be so dependent on others. Anne takes his blood pressure and temperature and moves back over to the operating list to write up her notes. A few minutes later she returns and asks the son whether his father usually has high blood pressure or if he is especially anxious about the operation. The son says that his father is particularly worried about when he will be able to see again. Anne explains a bit more about the timing, saying again that initially he will only be able to see a bright light, but that after a couple of hours he will be able to see shapes, and tomorrow morning his sight should be OK. Leaving the patient, she walks back over to the operating list and passes on this information to another nurse standing there, saying that his blood pressure is high and that he is feeling stressed. Sister Karen jokes with the nurses about having to find a replacement pair of pyjamas for a nurse, as she has given a pair to the patient, and, laughing as she walks off, she says that she hopes she can find a pair big enough.

The patient's anxiety about the operation was quickly moved away from and shut out by the nurses, the joke providing another way out of the tension and a defence against the depressive feelings and anxieties which were felt as too difficult to bear. With little or no privacy, any show of emotion in front of strangers may feel unbearably exposing for the patients, and for the clinical personnel emotional displays of anxiety and vulnerability by patients may give rise to intense feelings of guilt, and a desire to escape from them.

I observed only one open display of upset, during my sixth observation:

A teenage girl of about 16, accompanied by her mother, emerges after a private assessment with the anaesthetist, her head buried in her mother's shoulder. The mother has her arms around her daughter, and is leading her to a chair. The dental surgeon, who has been waiting to see the patient, approaches, pulls up a stool in front of her, sits down and introduces herself. The girl looks up and I can see that she has been crying. Her mother explains that she's OK, but a little upset – she's never had anything like this done before. Jane, the assigned nurse, looking concerned, then walks over from the operating list to join them, crouching down beside the patient's chair. The surgeon is talking to the girl, and then Jane, leaning on the side of the chair, says that if she cries she'll start her off, and then her make-up will run and that would never do. She goes on to explain that she'll be there throughout the operation for any additional hugs that are needed. The dental nursing assistant also walks over and stands just behind the group, hesitantly. The mother asks about the possibility of going into theatre with her daughter. Jane explains that this isn't possible – looking at the dental surgeon for confirmation – but that she can go to the exterior room with her and give her a big hug before she goes into theatre. Jane then reiterates her comments about her make-up running, stands up and breaks away from the group. The dental surgeon gets up too and walks back to the operating list, leaving her assistant standing there looking rather uncomfortable. The mother looks up at him and says that her daughter is OK and won't bite. He sits down on the stool and starts to ask his questions. I look over to the other young female dental patient who is on her own and looking anxious. She seems to be finding it hard to concentrate on her book. I feel a sense of isolation, wanting to go and give her a hug. Suddenly I become aware that all the nurses have disappeared from the area.

In the face of this non-uniform demand, the nurses and clinical personnel seemed unsure of what to do and unable to adapt to this unfamiliar situation. Jane's comments to the patient about her make-up seemed to reflect her difficulty in dealing with the distress being projected into her, which threatened her well-functioning façade. In order to keep the façade (make-up) intact, the disturbing feelings had to be pushed away, and when she was unable to get the patient to identify with her own mode of functioning, she had to distance herself from the intensity of the emotion and the dangerous feelings of distress, as did the other nurses.

It seemed that for the staff working in the day case unit and having to deal with such exposure, lack of privacy and the constant intrusions and confrontations with mentally painful experiences, anxiety could not be tolerated and had to be shut out of the space, both mentally and physically. The space limitations within the small and exposed assessment area meant that anxious patients were often physically removed, shutting any anxiety away from sight and mind, as if it was infectious.

DISCUSSION

I have attempted to give an account of my observations of the life and functioning of a day case centre which I observed weekly over a three-month period. By observing the events and interactions and my own emotional responses, I have tried to verify the place of these within the observation experience and to understand the observation from a psychoanalytic perspective. I have looked at the anxieties and conflicts stirred up in nurses and other staff by the nature of their work in the day case centre as well as those raised by my presence, and I have looked at the defences used, both individually and collectively, to deal with these anxieties. Although the nurses and other clinical staff in a hospital day case centre are not working with physically ill or injured patients, the brief but intense relationships with patients who are strangers and generally in good physical health can stir up painful feelings which can be difficult to think about. In this particular centre, the lack of personal privacy, constant intrusions, exposure to and continual confrontation with embarrassing and anxiety-provoking experiences increased the need to escape from the mental anguish.

Procedures such as undressing were often dealt with loudly and humorously, sometimes in rather an infantilising but sexualised way. Skogstad (1997) described how feelings aroused by close intimate physical contact with patients can be made less frightening by expressing them in light and humorous ways, whilst erotisation also provides a defence against depressive anxieties. However, in a day case centre the physical closeness exists in the absence of any emotional closeness. The intrusion into people with whom there is no chance to develop any real contact led, in this case, to an over-intrusiveness and a neglect of personal boundaries and privacy that sometimes felt embarrassing and at other times irritating. A denial of adult sexuality (particularly male) and the importance of personal privacy for the individual also seemed to provide an escape from the difficult feelings raised by the intrusive and intimate contact with strangers.

Rather than the fear of death itself (although this is always a potential risk) there was a fear of damage – fear of the impact caused by intrusive interventions into generally well-functioning bodies. This dilemma seemed to reflect my own anxieties about my role as observer and how to manage the feelings of intrusiveness into this ostensibly healthy and well-functioning organisational body. The nursing team also had to deal with the anxieties raised by the constant intrusions into their own physical and mental space. The erection of psychological boundaries provided a means by which the importance of the individual and the impact of the constant intrusions into others and oneself – the feelings of fear, resentment envy and guilt – could be denied. People were stripped of any individual identity, and patients had no personal privacy or place of their own, often being moved around during the assessment process which frequently resulted in the loss of their place to another. Menzies ([1959] 1988) described how the reduction of individual distinctiveness aided professional and personal detachment, by minimising the possibility of a relationship between individual personalities, and also how relationships were broken up by moving nurses. Skogstad (1997), in a study of a general hospital ward, also described how patients were frequently moved – as if objects without feelings.

Although the general atmosphere in the centre was usually very friendly and jolly, contact was often transient and restricted to when the process required it. Patients and clinical personnel seemed to move in and out of physical and psychological spaces almost as if making no impact. Skogstad (1997) observed how fleeting and superficial contact enabled troublesome feelings to be avoided, particularly those of loss. Donati (1989) referred to 'touch and go' contact, in a study of a chronic psychiatric ward, as a means of maintaining stereotyped and depersonalised relationships. The brevity of contact also seemed to reflect the brevity of the surgical interventions, as if everything had to be brief and frustrating just because the medical treatment was. My own attempts to move in and out without being noticed – to deny the impact of my intrusive presence in the organisational body –

seemed to reflect the attempts of the staff to deny the impact of their physical and psychological intrusion into one another's space and that of the patients. It was as if the organisational process had taken over and supplanted relations between people, perhaps because of the speed with which treatments were accomplished. When momentary interpersonal contact did occur it was transient and subverted into part of the process. The impact of my own 'strangeness' and intrusion as an observer into a culture where there was no room for individuality was dealt with by a denial of the individuality I represented and an attempt to change me into something more acceptable and less anxiety-provoking for the group.

My own desire to escape from any direct attention was reflected in the way that the nurses and clinical personnel seemed to use the exposed group setting and loss of individual distinctiveness as a means of preserving some anonymity and personal privacy – becoming just one of many – and thus avoid the anxieties implicit in direct contact between two individuals. Anxious patients were shut away separately and expressions of anxiety were often quickly moved away from, both psychologically and physically, thereby providing a means by which the anxiety could be shut out and reflecting my own desire to escape from anxiety and emotional anguish.

On the surface there was an atmosphere of comfort and harmony, reflected in the co-ordinated colours, finishes and furnishings, the neat, tidy and organised space and the generally jovial atmosphere. However, it seemed as if this façade was constantly being endangered by the underlying anxieties stirred up by the nature of the work, which were often shut off under the pressure of the mental pain. Given the ever-increasing pressure on NHS resources, the nature of the work in the day case centre, and the anxieties raised, were unlikely to be the only reasons for the shutting-off. However, the unconscious nature of these anxieties may go some way to explain the discomfort experienced by the staff and the difficulty they had in making sense of their feelings that the area didn't work as well as they would like.

One of the first comments made to me by the staff was about their dissatisfaction with the hospital gowns, being 'one size' only and often rather exposing. It would seem that they were intuitively looking in the right area when they expressed their concerns, which aptly reflected the problems I observed within the day case centre: depersonalisation and a lack of recognition of the individual, who may well be of 'different size', and the exposed nature of the centre where there was nowhere to hide.

Chapter 10

Sitting close to death

A palliative care unit

Noreen Ramsay

INTRODUCTION

Death is as natural a phenomenon as birth. Our society has become distanced from both. Increasingly death, like birth, has been taken over by medical specialists and removed from its place within the natural cycle of the family. This creates difficulties for the individual undergoing the private, personal experience of the process of dying within a medical setting. It also creates difficulties and challenges for those professionals caring for them.

In the last 20 years the development of the Hospice movement came with a recognition that hospitals concerned with giving acute medical care did not enable people to die with dignity and respect. In hospitals with a primarily diagnostic and curative attitude, dying was seen as a failure. Palliative care developed as a patient centred approach to physical, psychological and spiritual healing, its primary aim being the relief of distressing symptoms in order to allow the person to make the best possible use of whatever life they have left, potentially enabling the process of dying to be one of personal growth (Saunders 1960). I was initially attracted as a junior doctor to the ideas of the hospice philosophy because of their recognition of the impact of patient care on the professionals working with the dying patient. This understanding was blatantly lacking in my experience of acute general medicine.

With the recognition of palliative medicine as a speciality in medicine and the rapid growth of services for the dying in the health service, a growing number of professionals are involved with the dying. Working so closely with the reality of death stirs up anxieties that need to be defended against, in order not to be overwhelmed by them. These defences may be helpful in enabling professionals to continue to offer something useful to dying patients. The palliative care unit as a whole will develop its own defensive system in order to reduce the level of anxiety of those working there. Like all defences, this system may be helpful, but may also develop in such a way as to hinder the primary task of patient care. Menzies ([1959] 1988) described a similar process in a paper which looks at the development of nursing practices. The influence of defensive dynamics on the working practices of a unit are not always recognised.

THE WARD OBSERVATION

As a psychiatrist I became involved in liaison work in a hospice and worked with medical teams in the care of patients dying with Aids. While I knew I had an interest in this area, I was apprehensive about pursuing it further without being able to answer questions about its personal impact. It is difficult to answer these questions while one is busy in a unit, taking an active part in the dynamics of the situation oneself.

I thought that the opportunity to do a ward observation of a palliative care unit would enable me to observe the functioning of the unit. In fact, I became more aware of my own defences. The palliative care unit I observed was in a separate building on the site of a district general hospital. The main work of the team was community based and therefore not accessible to me. The 25 in-patient beds were used for terminal care, assessment and relief of intractable symptoms and respite care. The unit was primarily nursing-led with lesser input from medical staff. It had been in existence for about eight years.

The ward observation was structured so that I sat in the corridor of the unit, in the same place, at the same time, for one hour a week, over 12 weeks. I wrote up my observations afterwards and discussed them in a fortnightly supervision. The method of observing and the function of such a seminar are described in more detail in Chapter 2.

ISOLATED BY PRIVACY

In the first few observation sessions my initial impression was of isolation. This was emphasised externally by the concrete structures. The unit was separate from the main building of the general hospital. It was not easy to walk between the two. I was told the building was originally designed as an isolation unit, only later being taken over as a hospice. For security reasons the front door was locked, a buzzer system being used to gain admittance. The effect of this arrangement was that those with terminal illness, while in the same grounds as the general hospital, were effectively isolated from it. Within the unit itself the emphasis was on privacy. The majority of the patients' rooms were private single rooms, with the only double rooms being occupied by patients who were not actually dying. Many of the doors were shut or left ajar. Each door had a notice which either said 'Do not disturb' or 'Knock before entering'. During a period when some of the patients were being barrier-nursed because of infection, this was changed to 'Do not enter, ask a staff member before entering'.

The only public area, the communal day room, was remarkable in its lack of use. Patients used it mainly to speak on the telephone, and staff used it for formal meetings. The only patient who seemed to inhabit this area regularly was an elderly lady who stood out from the other patients because of her air of independence and liveliness as she pushed herself around in her wheelchair. New patients, unsure of their place in the unit, made brief exploratory excursions into the corridor or day room, and then retreated to their rooms. The kitchen area was used mainly by relatives to do practical tasks such as making tea or washing up cups.

As an observer seated in the corridor I was aware of my position in the public space, which was at times dead quiet. All the life and all the dying was going on in the rooms, which were closed off and inaccessible to me. On my introduction to the unit I was shown all around the building and introduced to many of the staff and the unit cat. I was not shown a patient's room and did not meet any patient – 'for obvious reasons', I was told. Even the nursing staff hesitated to enter those rooms without some form of permission. They responded to a request for help from a patient by answering a 'call light' very quickly, but still knocked before entering the room. They glanced into rooms as they went along the corridor, or peered through the shutters on the door windows without opening a closed door and did not enter unless help was obviously needed. Volunteers were similarly tentative when offering their services. My own experience of this respectful distance and unwillingness to intrude was that the few people who approached me usually made a tentative enquiry as to whether I was waiting for someone or whether I wanted any tea. When I declined these offers there was no follow-up to my response and I was left alone. Despite an external appearance of openness and friendliness, there was the impression that something was being kept firmly locked away.

FACED WITH THE HORROR OF DEATH

Over the next three sessions I saw glimpses of the reality around me which I had felt isolated from. These images made me wonder what was going on in this place. The homely furnishings, mixed with hospital tea trolleys and oxygen cylinders, gave an appearance of the trappings of a friendly hospital with its routines and hierarchy of staff, busy going about their duties. Gradually I felt exposed to something much greater, more primitive and uncontrollable, in the face of which I was helpless.

Session 3

Throughout the earlier part of the session a baby was crying in one of the rooms and I sat wondering why the baby was there, why its mother was there and what was on her mind.

Towards the end, a family started to come out of one of the rooms further down the corridor and I thought I might be able to answer my questions, as they started to walk towards me. I was struck by a stiffness and formality in the way they all moved, particularly in the little boy of about four who seemed uncomfortable with his role of leading them down the corridor. It was more like a funeral procession than a walk to the day room to look for some toys to play with. Behind him was a woman in an electric wheelchair, whose young face and body were blown up to a grotesque size by the side-effects of steroids. Her legs dangled huge with swelling. She moved beside the pushchair where the baby wriggled in protest. A woman of similar age pushed the baby. She was thin, her face drawn taut, her body stiffly held upright. An older woman walked behind them, more at ease than the others.

They passed by me into the day room, making brief eye contact with me, asking the boy if he remembered where the toys were kept. They only stayed a few minutes, standing around awkwardly. The thin woman suggested they go somewhere else, a conservatory, where there would be toys and beanbags for the children. As they started to leave the unit, one of the nurses protested that the patient would freeze if she went out and insisted on getting a cardigan for her. They all waited stiffly in the corridor while the nurse got a rug for her shoulders and went back for another for her legs.

As I left the unit at the end of that session I glimpsed a man lying in bed. He saw me as I went by and raised himself onto one thin elbow and stretched out the other arm to me. 'Nurse', he called, eyes staring from his skull. I walked on and fled from my helplessness. During the week I was haunted by the images of his emaciated face, raised to me, and of the family walking down the corridor towards me.

Session 4

In the room nearest to me, a woman's voice was raised in response to gentle enquiries from her husband and son. She repeated 'yes, yes, yes, yes' in a loud monotonous tone to each enquiry. Not fully conscious, she struggled to maintain contact with them. Throughout the whole hour I listened to her voice.

A young man left the day room where he had been talking to an older couple and went into one of the rooms. Shortly afterwards he re-emerged with a young woman and they walked side by side, very slowly towards the day room. They paused to smile and comment on the damage done to the wallpaper by the cat. Her face rounded by steroids was still pretty and she was about the same age as I was. She glanced at me as she passed, but I could not maintain eye contact. I was too overwhelmed by the large ugly scar over her scalp, not yet concealed, where the hair was growing back on her shaven head.

An alarm call from one of the rooms sounded. No one responded. I sat and listened to it, becoming more and more anxious, wanting someone to do something, but feeling unable to act myself. It rang for several minutes.

Session 5

The night before the observation I had a dream about being in the unit. In this dream, I was in the corridor near to where I usually sat, but I was lying on the floor, being held up by my arms and feet by two nurses. My body was floppy and my limbs hung useless as a rag doll's as they tried to drag me along the floor. The feeling was of complete helplessness. Following this dream, I was apprehensive about what experience I was to be subjected to during this session.

I met the unit's black cat outside. This was unusual. Also unusual was that instead of his normally self-contained and independent attitude he came over to me looking to be stroked. I helped him to come through the door. The receptionist told me that he had been in and out about four times that afternoon and did not seem to know where he wanted to be. She said, 'We lost one today, he always senses it.' On the way down the corridor I passed an empty room with the bed made up and presumed this was the room where someone had died that day. There was an initial air of business on the unit, with people coming and going to the rooms. For the first time the fire doors were open in the day room. I was aware of a thin young Indian man sitting behind me in the day room reading a book and watching the corridor.

Then one of the nurses started closing the room doors and the shutters on the door windows in a brisk business-like fashion until all the corridor was sealed off. Only myself and the man behind me remained watching. The receptionist opened the doors at the other end and stood there, while the nurse remained in the middle of the corridor, both on guard. Two men in white coats wheeled a metal box on a trolley into one of the rooms and shortly afterwards came out and wheeled it off the unit. I felt for the other watcher. What must it be like to see this while sitting in vigil for a dying relative? The receptionist left her post and the nurse relaxed as she slowly went about the ward opening doors and windows. Gradually life returned to the ward. The nurses retreated into the staff room and discussed women's rights, etiquette and feminism. I sat, not quite able to believe what had happened.

The shuttering off of the ward was strongly reminiscent of the closing of curtains around beds on large wards when someone has died in a general hospital. It seemed an anxious attempt to shutter off from the reality of the death of a human being. The lack of acknowledgement left me isolated and wishing for the comfort of one of those cups of tea they were always offering. The only creature that expressed distress was the cat. One of the volunteers said she would go and let him in as he was howling outside. Later he went into one of the empty rooms and started ripping up the carpet with his claws. This place felt frightening. Beneath the veneer of a hospital it was a place where rituals were carried out involving the passage towards death, and the cat knew about it. There was something much older and more powerful, in the face of which modern medicine and my professional training were impotent – as I had been in my dream.

EXPOSED ALONE

In the following week I felt both anger and pain. The anger was at what I perceived to be a superficial response to another's suffering and the pain was for the isolation of a man dying alone.

Session 6

An older woman, small beside a tall grey-haired younger man, walked towards me, his arm around her shoulder.
'How are you doing, Amy?'
Somewhat hesitantly, her voice croaking, she said 'I'm doing all right.'
'You seem stronger today.' She did not look sure about this. 'Does Jack recognise you today?', he asked as they went past me.
The conversation continued, partly audible in the corridor while they made tea in the kitchen, her voice low and sad, while he spoke in a loud cheerful manner.
'It makes you think about mercy killing, but the doctors don't agree with it,' he said.
'While there's life there is still hope,' she replied.
'Not at this stage,' he answered.
'When you are married that long, they are part of your life.'
'I don't know, I've not been married that long.'
'He's 84.'
'We all have to go sometime.'
She said, 'Life goes on, but it's never the same again, you never get over it.'
'It depends what you mean get over it. When my father died I was really upset, but I had my life to live, I just got on with it.'
'When you are together 40 years they are part of you', she said.
'Did you meet Mrs S? Her husband died last week, very suddenly.'
'It's better like that,' she replied.
'Oh no, you don't have any warning, you feel cheated.'
'It's the monotony of just sitting there.'
'You don't want either really, do you? You are not used to it. You have never seen someone like this before? Your parents, when they died what age were they?'
'My mother was 69.'
'Did she collapse suddenly or get thin and die slowly?'

As I listened to the stream of clichés, discussing such major issues loudly, overheard by myself and the man repairing the telephone, I got more and more angry with his lack of contact with her suffering.

In the room nearest to where I sat, reserved for those patients needing most nursing care, was a man, Walter. Although I had never seen him, I had been aware of him in the earlier sessions because of the fact that he called the nurses frequently for help. When they went into his room, they seemed to have difficulty in understanding what he wanted, partly because of his deafness and partly because of his confusion. Over the previous two weeks, access to his room had become limited by a barrier-nursing policy which necessitated staff wearing rubber gloves and a face mask when entering his room. In the previous sessions he had not rung his call bell once.

This day I thought a lot about Walter during the observation. Again there was silence from his room. I was filled with a longing to go in and touch him. A nurse switched on the light in his room. The light switches were on the wall outside the rooms. I waited for someone to go in and be with him. I delayed my departure to see if someone would go in. No one did. His isolation was unbearable.

SHUTTERING OFF

In the weeks following Walter's death I found myself shuttering-off from the realities around me, much as the ward had been shuttered off for the removal of a body.

I had strongly to resist the urge to do something, to be busy or useful. It was particularly difficult when people were calling out for help and no one came immediately, to tolerate my role as an observer.

Once, a woman in the room nearest to me called out. It was a few minutes before the nurse came, to discover that she had fallen out of bed. I felt guilty and resented the role that kept me from responding.

I occupied myself by labelling people and assigning them roles as staff, patients, visitors, volunteers, in an attempt to make meaning out of the situation. I was comforted by familiar faces doing familiar routines, such as the regular appearance of the 'foot'-woman, who did her rounds with a basket and stool offering chiropody and manicures. When a label would not fit comfortably, I was disconcerted.

In one observation, I was shocked by a very young, very thin girl coming out of a room. My initial label was 'patient', but my mind rebelled and refused to think about this possibility and instantly reassigned her as a relative.

I became excited by the development of a philosophy about the place. The unit was named after a butterfly and the staff wore butterfly badges and logos. It had been explained to me that their philosophy was that although a patient's life in the unit may be brief it could be bright like that of a butterfly. Based on my observations I revised this. The rooms were cocoons, the patients were caterpillars, their bodies slowly disintegrating to undergo a transformation at death, into butterflies, the symbol of the spirit. This theory had me moving onto thoughts about the ideal environment for a caterpillar and how to supply it. Through these ruminations, I was protected from recognition of what was actually happening to the people in the unit.

I was reluctant to get emotionally involved again.

Another man was in Walter's room, and in the other room close to me, Salee, an Indian woman with a shaven head, who was unable to communicate verbally with the nurses, sat bolt upright in her bed, her back to the door. I did not want to think about what might be in her mind. I thought about the role of the cat in the unit for a whole hour. I felt sleepy and disassociated, lulled by the sound of the air conditioning.

When it came to writing up a final account of the observations I initially produced a scientific medical paper. On rewriting it, I found it emotionally difficult to give a detailed account of what I had seen and felt. It was not until I had done this that I came close to recognising the extent of my fear of helplessness.

IN TOUCH AGAIN

It was seeing warm human contact again that restored me. This also put me back in touch with the painful reality of dying.

Session 10

An Afro-Caribbean woman said goodbye to a visitor at the door of one of the rooms. She stood in her slippers, as she would at her own front door. After the visitor had left, she walked over to two of the nurses at the nurses' station and hugged each of them around the waist and, still with her arm around one of them, they talked. There was a smiling acceptance of the difficulties she faced as her husband lay dying, shared warmly between them.

A tall, thin, elderly man making his way back from a telephone call paused at the door of another elderly man who came out to speak with him. They exchanged a few details about their stay in the unit. Their isolation and physical frailty acknowledged, they tentatively arranged to visit each other's rooms later. The polite exchange held the companionship of meeting a fellow sufferer.

A young overweight Indian woman was accompanied into the corridor by her husband. He went to unfold the wheelchair outside her room. She shook her head and continued, walking painfully slowly with the aid of a walking frame. The frame marked the carpet as she dragged it along. The back of her night-dress was bloodstained. I felt angry. If they had to be in hospital, this couple belonged in a maternity unit, not here.

As I left, I had a glimpse of Salee, shaven headed, at the edge of her bed silently struggling to get out. Her bare legs tangled in the raised cot sides of the bed.

There was a wooden walking stick stuck into a bin outside the back door. Well worn, it had a slight crack. I took it with me wondering why it had been discarded and what had happened to the person who had owned it.

CONCLUSION: HOLDING THE BALANCE

During the weeks of the observation, I underwent a process. Initial anxiety, coupled with loneliness and isolation, as I found myself without the protection of my professional role and defences. The nightmare of helplessness in the face of the reality of death, followed by the pain of dying in isolation. Then I built the defences to protect myself again and shut off emotional contact. Only towards the end could I allow myself to get in touch again both with the pain and the human warmth of support.

This personal experience within one particular unit will not apply universally. Much of what I felt was my own personal reaction to being there. The overwhelming nature of the experience required a period of reflection to digest what I had been confronted with. I wondered, if this was the impact of being an observer on the unit for one hour a week what must it be like for those who worked there for many hours a day without any opportunity to reflect on what was happening to them. Some of what I had found myself doing, the urge to act, to label, to philosophise, in order to protect myself was reflected in the unit. The urgency to do something, to be of some use, was reflected in the business of the staff who rarely sat still, pacing the corridor vigilantly. They attempted to label me in various ways, usually anxiously enquiring as to whether I was waiting for someone.

One nurse who knew that I was there as an observer expressed how disconcerting my presence was. The presence of someone who was attempting to see what happened went against a culture where emotions were shuttered off. The unit had a philosophy of care which, while not of a specifically religious nature as in many hospices, was proposed as a model and was supported by butterfly badges and emblems. A tendency to cut off emotional reality was most marked in the manner in which the body was removed from the ward. It was also reflected in the lack of use of the day room as a communal room and in the emphasis on the privacy of the patients' rooms. These opportunities, offered by the culture of the unit for personal defensiveness, allowed the individual a retreat from the experience of being there and formed part of a social defence system.

Both staff and patients in such a unit are faced with the dilemma of maintaining warm human contact that truly expresses the reality of facing death, while at the same time keeping sufficient distance to prevent being overwhelmed by it. There needs to be an acknowledgement of the need for support, while maintaining a respect for privacy. This balance needs to be held by the patient according to his or her changing needs over time. The temptation is for it to be held by the staff, in some instances erring on the side of too much privacy, leaving the patient alone and isolated. In general, in a hospice the major issues of death and dying facing the patient and their family are very much on the agenda and are dealt with in a much more open way than in most hospital settings. However, the situation may be acknowledged and openly discussed, but the emotion connected with it remains 'shuttered off' or split off. The staff may find that in order to protect themselves from the distress of their close work with the dying they need to cut themselves off from the painful affects created by the situation. This may in turn leave them unable to make contact with patients who are struggling with the same difficulty.

Within the unit, these defences may have become part of the culture, making it difficult for staff or patients to exist outside of them. My own emotional development from being overwhelmed, to defensiveness, to being able to be more in touch again, may reflect a continual oscillation in the culture of the unit between procedural support, retreat into isolationist privacy and the emergence of a more sensitive contact. In a wider context, this particular unit may suffer from its close proximity to a district general hospital which may want to maintain the hospice as an isolation unit, thus splitting itself off from its dying patients. Moves towards more community based care and the integration of palliative care teams within the hospital setting may help to overcome some of these tendencies, but working with the dying will always stir up painful emotions and anxiety. Until professionals acknowledge the impact on themselves of working closely with dying patients, they are unlikely to recognise its impact on their clinical practice.

Part IV

Conclusions

Chapter 11

Reflections on health care cultures

R.D. Hinshelwood and Wilhelm Skogstad

It is clear from the write-ups of these studies that each of the observers did have a strong emotional reaction which, in some cases, clearly surprised the observer. Often the experience of finishing the observation was also a surprising wrench from the involvement. We conclude that the method is in itself a considerable success in its original purpose: to help people to become more aware of, or sensitised to, their own emotional relation to the settings they were in.

It could be argued that those subjective reactions are nothing more than the response to being an observer – an unnatural enough role – giving rise to unnaturally strong reactions. Nevertheless there was a considerable variation in the emotional states which the observers report. And this would suggest a significant other factor beyond simply the experience of the observer role.

There are presumably two possibilities for that other factor, one being the variation in the observers themselves. The role brings out something that is specific for the enduring mood or state of mind of that observer. This is most likely to be true, but we would argue that it is not the whole truth. For instance, despite the variation in the observations, there is also an element which is common in the experience of the wards in a psychiatric service (Chapters 3, 5 and 6); and those in the general hospital settings (Chapters 8, 9 and 10).

There is therefore some component of the observers' reactions which derives from the specific setting observed, and not merely solipsistic derivations of the observers' states of mind. One could say that there are two intertwined factors – the observer's personality and the organisation observed. Because of observer biases our conclusions must be cautious, and we look towards more studies of this nature. Nevertheless, to a significant degree these studies are already confirmatory of other reports. We knew that general hospitals working with physically ill people brought out specific anxieties (Menzies [1959] 1988); and Hinshelwood (1987a) hypothesised that similar anxieties are inherent in the work with mentally ill patients.

CULTURAL ATTITUDES IN MENZIES' STUDY

Menzies' view of the anxiety was at a quite general level. She conveyed a general stimulation of the deepest levels of aggressive phantasies, and how these generated specific work practices which she called defensive techniques – the task-list system, the frequent abrupt movement of nurses between wards, the referring of trivial decisions up the hierarchy, the projection of irresponsibility onto juniors, and the uniformity of individuals expressed in nurses' actual uniforms, and the way patients are referred to by their disease or bed-number rather than by name.

Though Menzies does not formulate it quite in this way, the defensive techniques suggest certain reasonable, or rather pseudo-reasonable, assumptions; there seem to be two:

- If one remains emotionally distant from patients one won't feel anxiety on their behalf.
- If responsibility for decisions is passed to someone else, then one can never feel guilty.

These cultural assumptions or attitudes are shared amongst the nurses – and indeed taught to newcomers – despite being unconscious, or at least unexpressed. Implicitly these are expressed in the defensive techniques.

The fragmentation of the work and formation of task-lists in Menzies' nurses reduce the nurse–patient relationship to a minimum – the first cultural attitude above. And they contribute to the rather frantic atmosphere of pressured activity in which nurses have little time to talk to patients or relatives. Turning to seniors to take decisions ensures the observance of the second of the above attitudes. All this, as Menzies pointed out, gives a corresponding sense of being undervalued, and a deteriorating satisfaction in the work.

Thus we identify the cultural attitudes as the key link in this system. In one direction, they rest on the personal anxieties inflated by phantasies, and in the opposite direction they support defensive techniques. The defensive techniques enshrine the unconscious sets of attitudes (or implicit 'myths') that give plausible reasons (however unconscious) for the defensive techniques. The specific quality of relationships, and the forms of practice that the cultural attitudes promote, gives rise to the characteristic atmosphere that pervades an organisation. We have contended that the sensitivity to that atmosphere is an important access into the complex of anxiety, defence and culture. That sensitivity is the tool used in the current observational work.

THE CULTURE OF MENTAL HEALTH CARE

The observation studies of mental health organisations indicate certain similarities to the defensive techniques in general hospital nursing. There tends to be an emotional distancing. However, the methods for achieving this distance (the defensive techniques), the anxiety, and the underlying cultural attitudes which appear to dominate the ward are all different in the mental health settings. We will now look at the finer distinctions that exist between the sets of cultural attitudes in different mental health settings.

A chronic psychiatric ward

Donati (Chapter 3) was very struck by the ambiguous 'touch-and-go' techniques in the way staff related to patients, and she described them very clearly. Given the nature of mental illness it is not possible so easily to divide the list of tasks as in the care of the physical body. An approach to someone with a mental illness must be to approach a person whose suffering is in some sense located in their personhood. Distraction into attending to the body or a part of it is not such an available option.

More than this, though, there seems to be a significant difference in the anxiety. While on the general medical ward the critical anxiety is the fear of someone dying; this is not so evident in a psychiatric setting. Here, the fear is of madness. One could say that madness is a kind of death of the mind. And indeed some of the care seems to be devoted towards bringing to life aspects of the person – especially their social interests, which often seem to have succumbed. However, it was striking that these efforts by staff to enliven the social life of the ward, and the interpersonal relatedness, were continually defeated by the staff themselves. This was remarkable, and seemed to be motivated by a fear founded on an attitude to life, rather than to death. Hinshelwood (1989) postulated, in connection with the Donati study, that one unexpressed cultural attitude took the form of the myth:

- Any lively interaction will lead to outbreaks of madness.

Liveliness is feared – not death. This then followed through into the specific forms of practice which Donati emphasised – the 'touch-and-go' kind of interpersonal contact, expressing the fear of ongoing dialogue between patients or between patients and staff.

The canteen in the mental hospital

This fear of some sort of madness flaring up was carried over into the canteen (Chapter 4). There the observer was excruciatingly aware of that anxiety, and the need to 'police' it, as he observed. An almost totalitarian sense of control was in the air, and to his consternation it could even be expressed in terms of his own rigid 'steel castle' which he had built around himself. In this sense, the anxiety takes a slightly different form from the Donati study. Rees's observations in the canteen were conducted in a setting in which the patients' appetites were expressed and satisfied. The typically bleak but safer form of deadness, achieved on the ward, could not be sustained in the canteen where patients had to indulge in a full meal. It was of course bodily care, and the canteen culture seemed to reduce it very much to the formalities of bodily feeding. However, there was a very strong sense, it seemed, that such bodily appetites could spread to become uncontrolled psychic interactions that then forecast madness. It could therefore be hypothesised that the canteen culture expressed the following attitude:

- Allowing the pursuit and satisfaction of appetites can threaten mad interaction.

One could imagine that this 'myth' refines the previous one – that liveliness results in madness. Or, so to say, that appetites and life are felt at this unconscious level as much the same thing. Thus the canteen is a particularly risky setting, where 'life' and appetites must be allowed to become more intense for a brief controlled period. We might remember in this context how the feeding arrangements described by Donati were some of the most obsessionally controlled in the whole of her ward.

An admission ward

The care of the acute mentally ill, described by Chiesa (Chapter 5) was dominated by the experience of impotence. He described how the admission ward was left to handle those problems which were found to be too much for society and other parts of the psychiatric service to cope with. The ward staff, like the observer, were then filled with the powerful feelings of depression and hopelessness, uselessness and meaninglessness, and an angry futility as if their time was wasted. This impotence was not so dissimilar to that expressed by Donati's staff. However, here these distressing reactions to the work seemed to be much more on the surface. Chiesa stressed the possibility that any defensive system might have been weakened by the recent changes in psychiatric provision, and he seemed to confirm this.

Nevertheless, the culture did seem to express certain attitudes that had not been properly thought through and were therefore likely to draw on unconscious sources. There was a particular passivity about the initial contact by the observer – as if the idea of an admission ward was to admit anything, including the observer. In addition, the staff expressed this attitude again when a patient dropped a tray of glasses: without comment the nurses simply cleared up the mess. That vignette with the dropped glasses expressed an overriding sentiment – that staff were merely there to accept and to clear up any mess. Compared with the long-stay ward, the idea of preventing a mess (madness) from occurring had faded, and the mess of patients – their madness – was simply to be cleared up when it happened. There was a despairing attitude:

• The job is simply to clear up whatever others do and drop here.

This attitude was in important ways unthought and uncritical. It did not allow any thought about who might be admitted – including real interest in an observer and whether s/he could be coped with in the light of the obvious pressure. Nor could there be thinking about who cleared up the mess. Clearly staff had a responsibility for attempts to deal with mad outbursts, but presumably even on a hard-pressed admission ward some patients could handle clearing up a physical mess (certainly if some could help with managing the glasses in the first place).

Rehabilitation

The radical changes in psychiatric provision referred to by Chiesa affected the long-stay wards as well. Edwards (Chapter 6) conducted her observations on such a ward nearly a decade after Donati's study. At this time the wards were no longer segregated, and there was a strong ethos that patients were to move to the world outside. The sense of the ward or the hospital as a sealed unit that might be present in Donati's study was no longer there. The impact of the ward atmosphere on the observer was quite severely debilitating of thought and reflection.

Edwards had to struggle long and hard after her observations were completed in order to gain some clarity about her experience. This was reported in several of the studies, but in hers she took a particular interest in that process of regaining one's own capacity to think and give meaning to one's experiences. Interestingly, she captured meaning for herself in the sense of 'space' and 'place'. Of course, this may have been a serendipitous use of the theories of Winnicott and Milner; but, it did show a remarkable correspondence to the issues that the ward faced – the place patients had, and the uncertainty whether that place was in the ward or outside in the community. This occupied so many of these rehabilitating patients. Like in the admission ward, there seems to have been a remarkable change in the system of the long-stay ward in which the anxiety had begun to leak around the edges of the unsettled defences. The upsurge of confusion and disorientation in the observer seems to have related to the unsettled lives of the long-term inmates.

Unsettling incidents amongst the patients were frequently observed, and these often seemed to be dealt with by minimal intervention of staff – compared with so many other observation studies. The slightly more self-contained nature of the patients in this study was often acutely painful to the observer. The staff's distance seems to have been much more of a physical kind, leaving the patients in the day room to cope themselves. It all seems to have been part of an implicit assumption about the boundary between inside people (the patients) and outside people (the staff, the window-cleaners on one occasion, and the observer). It is as if there was an assumption about the patients' 'place' in the hospital, an assumption that could be expressed as follows:

- Patients are to be seen as independent people who have a place in the ward so long as they are leaving, i.e. not having a place.

This may be realistic, in a sense, for a hospital intent on discharging into the outside world as many of their patients as possible. However, like other cultural attitudes, it appears to have been unthought. In the form expressed above the ambiguity is apparent. This seems to have been unrecognised, and especially the profound disorientation that seems to have been experienced but not expressed. Goffman (1961) also noted this kind of paradox in mental institutions.

Community care

Whilst the mental hospitals have been decanting their less acutely disturbed patients, the 'community' has been receiving them. Morris (Chapter 7) was interested in this 'other side', the community which now complements the hospitals. Although the observer was prepared for community care not being the ideal answer that it is sometimes rhetorically announced as, the intensity of his experience and distress in the culture of a social services hostel was considerably greater than he expected.

Clearly, the hostel saw itself in a different light from psychiatric institutions, and this was partly at the root of his reception as a psychiatrist. However, there was a very profound antagonistic and destructive set of attitudes towards formal authorities of all kinds. The challenge which the hostel, and perhaps social services in general, mounted against medical psychiatry seemed to give a licence to attack order and even perhaps sanity within the hostel itself. This was interestingly brought out in the observer's first contact as a story explicitly describing envious attacks on the breast. Repeatedly, the observations demonstrated a complete disregard for the ordinary gestures of community – no one could take responsibility for people arriving, there was no knowledge of the timetable of meetings, only a tiny proportion attended meetings, and respect for each other and the staff was more or less completely missing. In place of this missing community (in 'community care') was a vicious dominance of the strongest and most brutal.

One could capture this culture in the following assumption:

- People who have been in need of psychiatric care will recover best if removed from that care altogether.

Again, put in this self-contradictory form, this attitude conveys that it has not been thought through. The observer's alarm and distress is not just at this unconscious acceptance of the assumption, but at the consequences of it that are not addressed either – an alarm also that there seems to be no one capable of altering these consequences, even if they are consciously debated.

THE CULTURE OF GENERAL HEALTH CARE

We have been struck by the variety of cultural atmospheres that can be expressed in the form of phantasies about the condition of mental illness and its treatment. In moving on to the studies of organisations set up to deal with physical illness we believe that these studies confirm the general conclusions to Menzies' classic study. We are, however, able to compare three separate settings.

The general hospital ward

Skogstad's study (Chapter 8) offers a chance of looking once again at the setting which Menzies originally studied (but with this very different method). In this case the observer found himself noting just the kinds of emotional distancing that were originally reported. The observer felt in the centre of great activity. He found it very difficult to witness the emotional neglect of patients, expressed often in their abrupt movement around the ward or to elsewhere. Relations with patients often appeared mechanical.

However, Skogstad's observations give some specific insights into the culture of his particular ward. At times staff did recognise the distress of their patients, but this was coped with in a manner reminiscent of Donati's 'touch-and-go'. The staff's own distress was less often attended to, being hidden behind a cheeriness which encroached upon the erotic. There was an enduring surface friendliness, which was also very transitory and seemed shallow. The demand for friendliness seemed to rule out all other feelings, such as pity, despair, anger, fear, which are its antithesis. The particular demand for a friendliness-in-adversity seemed to him an unfair demand on patients and left them in a state of isolation and further loneliness.

Skogstad refers to this as a manic culture, and it is certainly true that the despair found in psychiatric care, was not nearly so evident. The sense of inadequacy came through in more subtle ways – the flat battery in one observation, the sadness at giving up patients to another unit for specialist tests and care, and the continual sense of not enough staff or beds. At the same time there appears to have been an intrusiveness into the privacy of patients – their emotional states seemed to be open to the public corridors, as were their rooms. Like the physical care which demands an open access to their bodies through natural or surgical apertures, their emotional states were unthinkingly exposed. There was a functional in–out quality of bodily care as nurses attended to the patients' physical illnesses, which transposed into a similar in–out emotional quality.

In this culture there seem to have been certain underlying assumptions, which remain unexamined:

- If enough friendliness is generated, then fear, anxiety and pity won't have to be felt.
- Busy activity is the antidote to, or mastery of, death.

In physical care there is, perhaps understandably, even less thoughtful attention to the emotional and relational aspects of the treatment setting, as the physical body takes precedence.

Day surgery

Pressures on resources have demanded reductions in length of stay in hospitals for physical as well as mental care. One increasingly common solution is day care surgery for minor conditions. Maxwell observed a specially built unit for such a service (Chapter 9). There was considerable pride amongst the staff, and a good deal of thought had been given to designing the throughput of patients in the physical space. However, there was a very considerable sense of distress in the service, without the staff being aware of its source. The observer was very occupied by a painful sense of exposure, both physical and personal. She witnessed considerable embarrassment in patients, and also in herself. A good deal of effort went into the assessment of the patients, this involving undressing bodily and sometimes very public interviews of patients. Patients' personal anxiety and distress at the procedures they faced were not necessarily allowed any privacy. This is very similar to the acute ward that Skogstad observed.

In some ways this suggests a callous insensitivity on the part of the staff, and they pursued the work as if on a conveyor belt system. However, there were moments of significant contact – some very emotional. These moments were brief and could be terminated abruptly. The impact of brief surgical interventions on patients appeared to influence the momentary relationships that developed too, and is enhanced by the fact that it is a day service, not in-patient.

The brief but intense moments of contact were quickly terminated – particular upsets soon became interruptions; and in general they were supplanted by a briskly efficient conveyor system. The observer repeatedly describes her own wish to vanish from the scene. And a mechanical conveyor belt system allowed staff to disappear emotionally into a set of mechanical roles and functions that compose the process. This attempt at efficiency left the idiosyncrasies of individuals exposed – clothes were not the right individual sizes, persons followed in the track of case files, and punctuality was very strict. This added a poignant depersonalisation to the already brief personal contacts. Though the defensive techniques were different, the depersonalisation that Menzies described remained.

The atmosphere of energetic bustle, with callous disregard for personal individuality, seemed to reflect an underlying attitude:

- If quick surgical interventions give efficiency, then similarly transient personal contact will be most efficient too.

This brisk efficiency connects with a similar experience in Skogstad's acute cardiology ward. Although in this day centre there seems to have been some thought about the emotional contact, it was apparently dealt with by regulation into a conveyor system which allowed personal and emotional distress and relational contact only in a specified and planned way.

Interestingly the staff in this observation explicitly told the observer of their sense of something wrong, but still the capacity for sensitively thinking about it was strangled.

Death itself

As the anxiety about death is central to a hospital's work, its terminal care hospice represents the most poignant of its units. Ramsay's observation in the hospice (Chapter 10) started with the expectation that acceptance of death is an important function for medical and nursing staff. However, her observations led her to conclude that the form of that acceptance was much distorted, in a way that created considerable further distress. The observer writes painfully about the sense of helplessness, but does not exactly complain of impotence. It is the helplessness to approach another in need. The setting dealt with death by isolating death, in the most concrete terms – the isolation unit, the single rooms, the closed doors, and the emptiness of the 'communal' room. It was an emotional isolation in which distress was 'shuttered off', and only the cat seemed to retain the basic responses to the atmosphere.

That personal isolation was reflected, too, in the cognitive responses. There was overt recognition of death and of the need for human support in patients and relatives. But the recognition was a surface one, leaving sequestered the emotional pain of wanting to relieve them whilst not being able to stem the remorseless oncoming moment. The relentlessness of death seemed to provoke a similar relentless process of dealing with it.

There was a very clearly expressed cultural pattern here. The attitudes recognised death and human needs around it. However, as in the acute cardiology ward, there was a philosophy of stoical brightness, of shining through like a colourful butterfly – not in this instance so obviously erotic. On the surface, a brisk brightness covered a set of unconscious attitudes:

- Helplessness in the face of death can be avoided by isolating the experience of death.
- Surface brightness can dispel the terrifying darkness of death.

Given the expressed pain of the dying and their relatives, regulation of death in this way redoubled the isolation and increased the helplessness. The lack of thought about these consequences suggests once again that the attitudes were driven by hidden unconscious sources.

OBSERVING THE ATMOSPHERE

In general the mental health institutions seemed to adopt specific attitudes to anxieties, mostly focused around despair and impotence, that derived from a particularly self-defeating attitude to life: that life is akin to madness. In those organisations dealing with physical illness, the cultural attitudes deal more freely with personal contact, giving rise to quite a variation in the defensive techniques employed.

We have described something we call the culture, sets of attitudes which can be felt as the 'atmosphere' of the organisation. There is a chain of events: anxieties lead to defence mechanisms which are collectivised as socially transmitted sets of attitudes which support defensive techniques. Those attitudes emerge as actions and relationships which give rise to a characteristic, palpable atmosphere in the organisation. In practice, however, we expect observational work to proceed in the opposite direction. The detection of the atmosphere leads to a reflective thoughtfulness about it and then to hypothesise the defences and anxieties behind the atmosphere.

On the whole these observations have been successful in creating an interest in organisational dynamics, and in sensitising people who will eventually have formal authority in the culture of organisations that function to care. However, there are many problems with this method as research: over-interpreting, pre-existing theory and circular proofs, observers' non-theoretical prejudices, and the smallness of the observers' keyhole visions. These are all too obvious. At the same time we would claim that the intensity of the culture, its anxieties and its unaddressed assumptions, cannot be gained so quickly or starkly in any other way. The observer's emotional sensitivity is a unique kind of probe. The research use to which we have put these studies cannot in our view be dismissed. There is a striking confirmation of the Menzies studies on the defensive techniques of a general hospital nursing service. And we would claim that there is some considerable internal consistency within these observations which suggests we are not merely seeing observer anxiety and bias.

Much of the readers' reactions might be that certain things should be done differently by the staff in the observed wards and organisations. Even though that may be justified, this was not the aim of these studies and is not the purpose of presenting them. Instead the question we ask is different: Why are things actually done this way, when, with objective thought, they might be done better? Our assumption is that there is an answer to that question. There are reasons why things are done the way they are and why clear thinking is obstructed in certain areas. Those reasons have power behind them – the power of unacknowledged or even unconscious anxieties. Our purpose has been to try to give a keyhole view into seeing those unseen emotional reasons, the deep anxieties and the multiple ways of defending against them.

It is important to remember that these studies were training exercises with, when gathered together, a superimposed research function. They were not attempts to change the systems which were studied. This places our studies in contrast to those of Obholzer and Roberts (1994), whose work was discussed in Chapter 1. Their results were gained from a consultancy method which *did* have the task of bringing about change, and their studies display some significant differences.

CONSULTANCY TO HEALTH CARE SYSTEMS

Obholzer and Roberts's method of change was to attempt to introduce 'external' thinking into the organisation. This attempt to get thinking going in these gaps contrasts with our method of getting into the culture and simply experiencing it.

Our focus on describing the culture and the underlying anxieties and defences is a different perspective. We are able to move aside from the tension we discovered in the Obholzer and Roberts work between a more psychoanalytic focus on anxieties and defences and a more systemic one on the management system. We can therefore stick more closely to the psychoanalytic perspective and to Trist's original project. The importance of the Obholzer and Roberts work is to keep us focused on issues such as the task of the institution, its boundaries and the exercise of authority and leadership within it, which are important for introducing change and might be relatively overlooked in a purely psychoanalytic perspective.

The studies from the Obholzer and Roberts workshop exemplify these issues of task, boundary and authority/leadership; this, we believe, complements our study, which is more concerned with anxieties, defences and cultural attitudes.

Obholzer (1987, 1994a, 1994b) focuses particularly on authority and leadership as key aspects of organisational life. The leader needs to keep the organisation to the task, and to ensure that boundaries are effectively kept. Inevitably these elements of system maintenance are central – and their consultancy work is still reliant on systems theory. Those who call consultants into organisations tend to be the middle and senior managers, who are inevitably less close to the anxiety aroused by the primary task but worry instead about the maintenance of the system itself. The aim of consultants is to bring about change, and they therefore need to be much more concerned with those who can function as change agents. However, in focusing on the aspects of the system that are directly amenable to change they may sometimes miss out on some important aspects of the culture. Both these aspects are part of the organisation and need to be thought about in balance as complementing each other.

Although the studies in our book were not intended as consultation, it was striking that many, perhaps most, of the staff teams observed expected a useful report at the end of the observation, as if looking for help in their practice. And this no doubt expressed a felt need for more support. When it came to the end of the observations, there was never a demand made by the staff for a report – and when on one occasion the written-up study was sent to the staff, no response was gained. Of course, the team's lack of request does not necessarily mean that they were not in fact still interested. Rather, it seems the endings of the observations were so little remarked – or marked – by the team that the observer often felt a very painful sense of 'ships passing in the night'. All of the observations have indeed shown the need for much more of a culture of support for the workers and containment of their anxieties within health care organisations. The high level of defensiveness that was found in many of the observed institutions appeared to be linked with the apparent lack of containment of anxieties within the organisations.

We have tried to show the use of an observation method that is not burdened with responsibility for change of the observed organisation. It is a training use, but also we have drawn some research conclusions from it. Our studies have taken place over more than fifteen years, but they can be connected with a tradition of psychoanalytic accounts of organisations that stretches back to the 1950s. There is a consistency about the results of psychoanalytic work on health care institutions over that period. At the same time we might also plot, to some extent, certain trends in the unconscious life of organisations which come from policy changes in the provision of care in the British National Health Service since then.

Bibliography

Barron, C. (1987) *Asylum to Anarchy*. London: Free Association Books.

Barton, R. (1959) *Institutional Neurosis*. Bristol: Wright.

Berger, P.L. and Luckmann, T. (1971) *The Social Construction of Reality*. Harmondsworth: Penguin.

Bick, E. (1964) Notes on infant observation in psychoanalytic training. *International Journal of Psycho-Analysis* 45: 558–566.

Bion, W. (1959) Attacks on linking. *International Journal of Psycho-Analysis* 40: 308–315. (Reprinted 1988 in Bott-Spillius, E., *Melanie Klein Today*, Volume 1, London: Routledge.)

Bion, W. (1961) *Experiences in Groups*. London: Tavistock.

Bleuler, E. (1924) *Textbook of Psychiatry*. New York: Macmillan.

Bott, E. (1976) Hospital and society. *British J. Medical Psychol.* 49: 97–140.

Bott-Spillius, E. (1990) Asylum and society. In Trist, E. and Murray, H. (eds) *The Social Engagement of Social Science, Vol. I*, London: Free Association Books, pp. 586–612.

Chiesa, M. (1989) Psychodynamic and systemic approaches: some areas of convergence. *Free Associations* 14: 62–78.

Chiesa, M. (1993) At the border between institutionalization and community psychiatry: psychodynamic observations of a hospital admission ward. *Free Associations* 4, 2: 241–263. (Reprinted as Chapter 5 of this book.)

Cohn, N. (1994) Attending to emotional issues on a special care baby unit. In Obholzer, A. and Roberts, V.Z. (eds) *The Unconscious at Work*. London: Routledge, pp. 60–66.

Coid, J. (1994) Failure in community care: psychiatry's dilemma. *British Medical Journal* 308: 805–806.

Conolly, J. (1856) *The Treatment of the Insane without Mechanical Restraints*. London: Smith, Elder.

Conran, M. (1985) The patient in hospital. *Psychoanalytic Psychotherapy* 1: 31–43.

Dartington, A. (1994) Where angels fear to tread: idealism, despondency and inhibition of thought in hospital nursing. In Obholzer, A. and Roberts, V.Z. (eds) *The Unconscious at Work*. London: Routledge, pp. 101–109.

de Board, R. (1978) *Psychoanalysis of Organisations*. London: Tavistock.

Devereux, G. (1978) *Ethnopsychoanalysis: Psychoanalysis and Anthropology as Complementary Frames of Reference*. London: University of California Press.

Dobson, F. (1998) Open letter to Professor Thornicroft.

Donati, F. (1989) A psychodynamic observer in a chronic psychiatric ward. *British Journal of Psychotherapy* 5: 317–329. (Reprinted as Chapter 3 of this book.)

Fletcher, A. (1983) Working in a neonatal intensive care unit. *Journal of Child Psychotherapy* 9, 1: 47–55.

von Foerster, H. (1973) On constructing reality. In Preiser, W.F.E. (ed.) *Environmental Design Research*. Strondsberg: Dowden, Hutchinson and Ross.

Freud, S. (1909) Notes upon a case of obsessional neurosis. *Standard Edition*, vol. 10. London: Hogarth Press.

Freud, S. (1914) Remembering, repeating and working-through. *Standard Edition*, vol. 12. London: Hogarth Press.

Freud, S. (1921) Group psychology and the analysis of the ego. *Standard Edition*, vol. 18. London: Hogarth Press.

von Glaserfeld, E. (1984) An introduction to radical constructivism. In Watzlawick, P. (ed.) *The Invented Reality*. New York: Norton.

Goffmann, E. (1961) *Asylums*. London: Anchor Books Doubleday.

Golding, W. (1954) *Lord of the Flies*. London: Faber & Faber.

Harrington, J. (1988) Psychiatrists – an endangered species? *Bulletin of the Royal College of Psychiatrists* 12: 169–174.

Heald, S., Deluz, A. and Jacopin, P.-Y. (1994) Introduction. In Heald, S. and Deluz, A. (eds) *Anthropology and Psychoanalysis: An Encounter through Culture*. London: Sage.

Helman, C. (1981) Disease versus illness in general practice. *Journal of the Royal College of General Practitioners* 230: 548–552.

Hinshelwood, R.D. (1979) Demoralisation in the hospital community. *Group Analysis* 12: 84–93.

Hinshelwood, R.D. (1987a) The psychotherapist's role in a large psychiatric institution. *Psychoanalytic Psychotherapy* 2, 3: 207–215.

Hinshelwood, R.D. (1987b) *What Happens in Groups*. London: Free Association Books.

Hinshelwood, R.D. (1989) Comment on Dr Donati's 'A psychodynamic observer in a chronic psychiatric ward'. *British Journal of Psychotherapy* 5: 330–332.

Hinshelwood, R.D. (1993) Locked in role: a psychotherapist within the social defence system of a prison. *Journal of Forensic Psychiatry* 4, 3: 427–440.

Hinshelwood, R.D. (1994) Attacks on the reflective space – Containing primitive emotional states. In Schermer, V.L. and Pines, M. (eds) *Ring of Fire: Primitive Affects and Object Relations in Group Psychotherapy*. London: Routledge, pp. 86–106.

Hunt, J. (1989) *Psychoanalytic Aspects of Fieldwork*. London: Sage.

Jaques, E. (1953) On the dynamics of social structure. *Human Relations* 6: 10–23.

Jaques, E. (1955) Social systems as a defence against persecutory and depressive anxiety. In Klein, M., Heimann, P. and Money-Kyrle, R. (eds) *New Directions in Psycho-Analysis*. London: Tavistock, pp. 478–498.

Keenan, B. (1992) *An Evil Cradling*. London: Hutchinson.

Khaleelee, O. and Miller, E. (1985) Beyond the small group: society as an intelligible field of study. In Pines, M. (ed.) *Bion and Group Psychotherapy*. London: Routledge.

Lewis, I. (1977) Introduction. In Lewis, I. (ed.) *Symbols and Sentiments: Cross-cultural Studies in Symbolism*. London: Academic Press.

Main, T.F. (1975) Some psychodynamics of large groups. In Kreeger (ed.) *The Large Group*. London: Constable.

Menzies, I. ([1959] 1988) The functioning of social systems as a defence against anxiety. A report on a study of the nursing service of a general hospital. In Menzies Lyth, I. (1988) *Containing Anxiety in Institutions. Selected Essays Volume 1*. London: Free Association Books, pp. 43–85.

Menzies Lyth, I. (1990) A psychoanalytical perspective on social institutions. In Trist, E. and Murray, H. (eds) *The Social Engagement of Social Science, Volume 1*. London: Free Association Books, pp. 463–475.

Miller, E. (1993) *From Dependency to Autonomy: Studies in Organisation and Change*. London: Free Association Books.

Miller, E.J. and Gwynne, G.V. (1972) *A Life Apart*. London: Tavistock.

Miller, E.J. and Rice, A.K. (1967) *Systems of Organization: The Control of Task and Sentient Boundaries*. London: Tavistock.

Miller, L., Rustin, M., Rustin, M. and Shuttleworth, J. (1989) *Closely Observed Infants*. London: Duckworth.

Milner, M. (1950) *On Not Being Able To Paint*. London: Heinemann.

Obholzer, A. (1987) Institutional dynamics and resistance to change. *Psychoanalytic Psychotherapy* 2, 3: 201–205.

Obholzer, A. (1994a) Authority, power and leadership: contributions from group relations training. In Obholzer, A. and Roberts, V.Z. (eds) *The Unconscious at Work*. London: Routledge.

Obholzer, A. (1994b) Managing social anxieties in public sector organizations. In Obholzer, A. and Roberts, V.Z. (eds) *The Unconscious at Work*. London: Routledge, pp. 169–178.

Obholzer, A. and Roberts, V.Z. (eds) (1994) *The Unconscious at Work*. London: Routledge.

Orwell, G. (1945) *Animal Farm*. Martin Secker & Warburg.

Palmer, B. (2000) The Tavistock paradigm: inside, outside and beyond. In Hinshelwood, R.D. and Chiesa, M., *Towards a Psychoanalytical Social Psychology* (in preparation).

Perez-Sanchez, M. (1990) *Baby Observation: Emotional Relationships during the First Year of Life*. Perth: Clunie Press.

Pinel, P. (1801) *Traité médico-philosophic sur l'alienation mentale*. Paris.

Ramsay, N. (1995) Sitting close to death: observation on a palliative care unit. *Group Analysis* 28: 335–365. (Reprinted as Chapter 10 of this book.)

Rapoport, R.N. (1960) *Community as Doctor*. London: Tavistock.

Rees, J. (1987) Psychotherapy training: food for thought. *International Journal of Therapeutic Communities* 8, 1: 47–56. (Reprinted as Chapter 4 of this book.)

Reid, S. (ed.) (1997) *Developments in Infant Observation: The Tavistock Model*. London: Routledge.

Rice, A.K. (1963) *The Enterprise and its Environment*. London: Tavistock.

Rice, A.K. (1965) *Learning for Leadership*. London: Tavistock.

Roberts, V.Z. (1994a) Till death us do part: caring and uncaring in work with the elderly. In Obholzer, A. and Roberts, V.Z. (eds) *The Unconscious at Work*. London: Routledge, pp. 75–83.

Roberts, V.Z. (1994b) The self-assigned impossible task. In Obholzer, A. and Roberts, V.Z. (eds) *The Unconscious at Work*. London: Routledge, pp. 110–120.

Rosenberg, S.D. (1970) Hospital culture as a collective defence. *Psychiatry* 33: 21–35.

Rosenfeld, H. (1971) A clinical approach to the psychoanalytic theory of the life and death instincts: an investigation into the aggressive aspects of narcissism. *International Journal of Psychoanalysis* 52: 169–178.

Rosenhan, D.L. (1973) On being sane in insane places. *Science* 179: 250–258.

Rustin, M. (1989) Observing infants: reflections on methods. In Miller, L., Rustin, M., Rustin, M. and Shuttleworth, J., *Closely Observed Infants*. London: Duckworth.

Saunders, C.M. (1960) *Care of the Dying*. London: Macmillan.

Scott, D. and Starr, I. (1981) A twenty four hour family orientated psychiatric and crisis service. *Journal of Family Therapy* 3: 177–186.

Scull, A.T. (1977) *Decarceration: Community Treatment and the Deviant: A Radical View*. Engelwood Cliffs, N.J.: Prentice-Hall.

Selvini-Palazzoli, M., Anolli, L. and Di Blasio, P. (1987) *The Hidden Games of the Organization*. New York: Pantheon.

Sinanoglou, I. (1987) Basic anxieties affecting psychiatric staff and their attitudes to psychotic patients. *Psychoanalytic Psychotherapy* 3: 27–37.

Skogstad, W. (1997) Working in a world of bodies: defensive techniques on a medical ward – a psychoanalytical observation. *Psychoanalytic Psychotherapy* 11, 3: 221–241. [Reprinted as Chapter 8 of this book.]

Stanton, A.H. and Schwartz, M.S. (1954) *The Mental Hospital*. New York: Basic.

Trist, E. ([1950] 1990) Culture as a psychosocial process. In Trist, E. and Murray, H. (eds) (1990) *The Social Engagement of Social Science*. London: Free Association Books, pp. 539–545.

Trist, E. and Murray, H. (1990) Historical overview: the foundation and development of the Tavistock Institute. In Trist, E. and Murray, H. (eds) *The Social Engagement of Social Science*. London: Free Association Books, pp. 1–34.

Trist, E., Higgin, G., Murray, H. and Pollock, A. (1963) *Organisational Choice*. London: Tavistock.

VV.AA. (1998) PriSM Psychosis Study. *British Journal of Psychiatry* 173: 363–427.

Watzlawick, P. and Weakland, J.H. (1977) *The Interactional View: Studies at the Mental Research Institute, Palo Alto 1965–1974*. New York: Norton.

Winnicott, D. (1967) The location of cultural experience. *International Journal of Psycho-Analysis* 48, 3: 368–372.

Index